SPARED

A PATH TO FUELING HOPE AND QUENCHING PAIN

SPARED

A PATH TO FUELING HOPE AND QUENCHING PAIN

VIVIAN PELLAS

ethos
collective

SPARED © 2025 by Vivian Pellas. All rights reserved.

Printed in the United States of America

Published by Igniting Souls
PO Box 43, Powell, OH 43065
IgnitingSouls.com

This book contains material protected under international and federal copyright laws and treaties. Any unauthorized reprint or use of this material is prohibited. No part of this book may be reproduced or transmitted in any form or by any means, electronic or mechanical, including photocopying, recording, or by any information storage and retrieval system, without express written permission from the author.

LCCN: 2024927518
Paperback ISBN: 978-1-63680-447-7
Hardcover ISBN: 978-1-63680-448-4
e-book ISBN: 978-1-63680-449-1

Available in paperback, hardcover, e-book, and audiobook.

Any Internet addresses (websites, blogs, etc.) and telephone numbers printed in this book are offered as a resource. They are not intended in any way to be or imply an endorsement by Igniting Souls, nor does Igniting Souls vouch for the content of these sites and numbers for the life of this book.

Some names and identifying details may have been changed to protect the privacy of individuals.
FIRST EDITION: APRIL 2021
ISBN 978-958-5532-33-5

ALL PHOTOGRAPHS ARE REPRODUCED COURTESY OF
© Vivian Pellas, 2020

EDITORIAL DIRECTION
Leyla Bibiana Cangrejo Aljure

EDITORIAL PRODUCTION
Víctor Hugo Cangrejo Aljure

DIGITAL PRE-PRESS
Cangrejo Editores

PHOTOGRAPHY
Archivo Personal
Fotografía portada: Iván García
Fotografía de contraportada: Rodrigo Castillo

DESIGN
Sandra Liliana González B.

HISTORICAL RESEARCH
Salvador Espinoza Moncada

EXECUTIVE COORDINATION FROM NICARAGUA
Dennis Schwartz Arce

LOGISTICAL COORDINATION FROM NICARAGUA
Xiomara Argeñal Baltodano

TECHNICAL AND DOCUMENTARY SUPPORT
Grethel Guevara

TRANSLATION
Shehla Turner
Intercontinental Translations, Inc.

PHILOLOGICAL REVISION
Debra Nagao

To my dear parents,
Lydia García de Fernández and José Fernández
In memoriam

To my adored children,
Carlos Francisco, Vivian Vanessa, and Eduardo
The angels of my life

To my grandchildren,
Vivian Isabella, Juan Carlos,
Sienna Nicole, Nicolás, Pietro,
Joaquin, Valentina, and Lorenzo
The joy of my days

To Carlos, my beloved,
The inspiration of my life

CHILD
I will shelter you with my hair
And in the air will I seek a balm
that mitigates the pain

And if the fire rages,
I will quench it with my tears.

Vivian Pellas

**Poem by Vivian Pellas, which embodies her legacy of love
for the burned children of Nicaragua and the world.
The poem was engraved on the inaugural plaque of the first burn unit of the
Fernando Vélez Paiz Hospital in Managua in 1992.

CONTENTS

Dedication	5
Poem	7
Introduction	15
Foreword	19

PART I

Chapter 1	The Cuba of My Childhood	27
Chapter 2	My First Farewell	39
Chapter 3	Nicaragua: A New Beginning	51
Chapter 4	Carlos Pellas: My Destiny	65
Chapter 5	Earthquake in Managua: 6.3 on the Richter Scale	75
Chapter 6	Changing Horizons	81
Chapter 7	Happiness Knocks at My Door	89
Chapter 8	A New Life	97

Chapter 9	Reliving the Past	105
Chapter 10	The Exodus, a Ghost behind Us	113
Chapter 11	Mother Teresa of Calcutta, Premonition or Coincidence?	129

PART II

Chapter 12	An Inexplicable Fear	135
Chapter 13	"What a Nice Day to Fly!"	143
Chapter 14	Flight 414: An Encounter with Death	147
Chapter 15	An Angel on the Mountain	159
Chapter 16	Skinless	165
Chapter 17	"My Child, What Happened to You?!"	171
Chapter 18	"They Are Alive!"	185
Chapter 19	"I'm Dying"	193
Chapter 20	A Grand Master Called Pain	203
Chapter 21	And I Stopped Crying …	211
Chapter 22	"I Want to See My Children!"	227
Chapter 23	For the Children of Nicaragua	231
Chapter 24	A Suffocating Mask	239

| Chapter 25 | The Tortuous Legal Path | 247 |
| Chapter 26 | Life through Fire | 255 |

PART III

Chapter 27	Back to Nicaragua	265
Chapter 28	Finding the True Meaning of My Life	269
Chapter 29	Every Path Has Its Puddle	273
Chapter 30	An Unexpected Answer	281
CHAPTER 31	APROQUEN: The Divine Mandate!	285
Chapter 32	Not Expecting Anything in Return	293
Chapter 33	A Queen Arrives from Mexico	299
Chapter 34	A Dream Come True	303
Chapter 35	A World of Darkness and Isolation	309
Chapter 36	And Love United Us ...	315

PART IV

| Chapter 37 | An Irreplaceable Human Being | 325 |
| Chapter 38 | The Burden of Loneliness | 331 |

Chapter 39	"Here I Am ... My Ballerina"	339
Chapter 40	A New Sign	345
Chapter 41	And If the Fire Rages ...	349

Epilogue 357

APPENDICES

Testimonials of Those Who Have Shared This Path	363
Recognitions	377
Hall of Honor for Our Donors	389
Illusions, for our Children, Year after Year	393
My Life in Images	395
My Immense Gratitude ...	422

Prayer of Gratitude 427

On October 21, 1989, airline TAN SAHSA's Boeing 727-200, registered as N88705, was a passenger flight en route from San José, Costa Rica, to Miami, with stops in the cities of Managua, Nicaragua, and Tegucigalpa, Honduras. At 7:53 in the morning, the plane crashed into Cerro de Hula as it approached the Toncontín International Airport in Tegucigalpa.

135 people died.

Of the 146 passengers on Flight 414, only 11 people survived. Vivian Pellas is one of them. This is her testimony of how she returned from the brink of death and how it changed her life forever as she came to understand the mission she had to fulfill.

*They say that when you want to write your life story,
the blank page calls for the movie
of your life to start.
Then ...
you dust off your fears and count your scars,
including those of your body,
as well as those of your soul,
you tear them open and pick at them
until they bleed again.*

*I've asked myself many times,
why did all of this happen?
What was the purpose of experiencing
what I went through?
Why was I the protagonist of a story
carved by pain?
Today, I know that happiness comes from following
your heart, and I found it in my family
and in the smile of a child.*

Foreword
CARLOS PELLAS

When Vivian placed the final text of her autobiography in my hands, and as I became the first reader of this chronicle, I never imagined she would tell her story in such a sublime way. When I finished reading the words that are now this book, with tears in my eyes, I understood why it took her twelve years to write it.

Reliving everything she went through in her life—from her exile from Cuba to the trauma of the plane crash, and considering the implications of the complex and extremely painful rehabilitation she had to endure—must have been, unequivocally, more than an arduous exercise; it was an utter challenge to her spiritual tenacity. Today, I fully understand . . . and I could not hold back the tears as I read all those passages of the book, which deeply moved me. They not only brought back the tortuous moments I went through but also made me remember how essential we have been to each other, and how, at the most difficult moments in our journey, we have always been together to support, comfort, and encourage each other, overcoming the challenges that life gives us and that catch us by surprise.

Vivian writes that I was always her inspiration, but the truth of the matter is she is the one who has inspired me. I have admired her strength and optimism since the moment I met her. Those values empowered her to overcome the hardship of her exile as well as many of the ordeals she has had to face since childhood. I was even more surprised by her strength as she embraced her new homeland: Nicaragua.

Witnessing her torturous rehabilitation sessions heartened me not to give up and to face the pain with the same courage and determination she did.

Vivian's life, which is depicted with simplicity and humility in her autobiography, is not only one of the most compelling stories I have ever read but also one of the most inspirational ever written. Many who face a tragedy in which they unexpectedly lose a loved one or are involved in an accident that leaves permanent wounds and critical aftereffects spend much of their remaining lives lamenting in bitterness, incapable of finding purpose for their existence.

As the reader will see in this narrative, Vivian's life has not been easy at all, but her optimism and ongoing determination have helped her overcome the obstacles in her path. These challenges have forged her extraordinary character, making her not only a woman with great self-confidence but also a woman with an enormous heart.

When I met Vivian, I fell in love with her immediately, and at that moment, I knew she was the woman I would spend the rest of my life with. Nevertheless, I have to admit I never imagined she would become the Vivian Pellas she is today.

It is admirable how even with her flesh raw and with multiple fractures, she muttered: "I'm going to build a burn unit for children in Nicaragua." Just at that moment, when anyone else would have been thinking about his or her own plight and extreme pain, she was already exploring her new reason for being, thinking about how to alleviate the suffering of others. She did not blame God for everything that was going on in her life. Quite the contrary: she was trying to find the divine plan He had devised for her.

On several occasions, Vivian was on the brink of life and death. I'm sure her love for our children and the fear of leaving them alone, the support of her parents, family members, and friends, and the magnificent work of the doctors and the nurse who took care of her were factors that helped her survive her precarious condition. However, the most important factor was, unquestionably, her unwavering faith in God!

Vivian was convinced that, behind all this personal tragedy, there was a mission God had in store for her. This faith filled her with strength, helped her withstand the colossal pain of the treatments and, essentially, transformed her life to pursue one cause: to create a world that is more compassionate, just, and inclusive for the thousands of children from low-income families that are severely burned in our country every year.

After witnessing what Vivian has accomplished through aproquen, a foundation dedicated to helping children suffering from burns in Nicaragua, God's mission for her couldn't be clearer: to make her the *Guardian Angel* of pediatric burn victims in Nicaragua.

No doubt Vivian's story will become an inspiration for many others to channel their efforts into creating a more tolerant, just, and benevolent world.

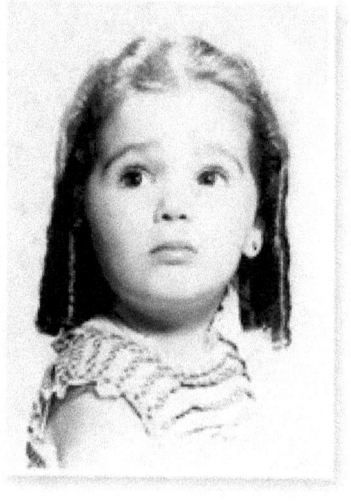

PART I

Our story
is precisely
that of ...
continuous
rebirth.

Mother Teresa of Calcutta

CHAPTER 1

Vivian at the age of two. Havana, Cuba, 1956.

The Cuba of My Childhood

I came into this world on March 5, 1954. I was born in the former "Quinta La Covadonga" Hospital in Havana, the same place where my brother was born. I was a joyful and vigorous baby. However, I had a problem in my pylorus: I would expel milk every time I was fed. Had it not been for the timely opinion of a doctor, who determined that the cause of my symptoms was nervous spasm, I would have needed surgery. Nonetheless, a few drops of medicine before the bottle cured me completely.

Even so, the truth is that, during my first months of life, I cried a lot and would not let my mom sleep.

Lydia García de Fernández, Vivian's mother. Havana, Cuba, ca. 1935.

The passing days and the baptismal water the priest sprinkled on my head at the Church of the Sacred Heart of Jesus eventually soothed my crying. I was baptized Vivian because when my mom was single, people in the street would ask her if she was Vivien Leigh, the actress who played the main character in the movie *Gone with the Wind*, which was very popular at the time. She was asked the same question so often that she decided if she ever had a daughter, that would be her name.

I started kindergarten when I was three. My mom said I was a fast learner. That is where I took my first ballet classes. It was my first introduction to dancing, a passion that would accompany me all my life and that saved me in the most trying times of my existence.

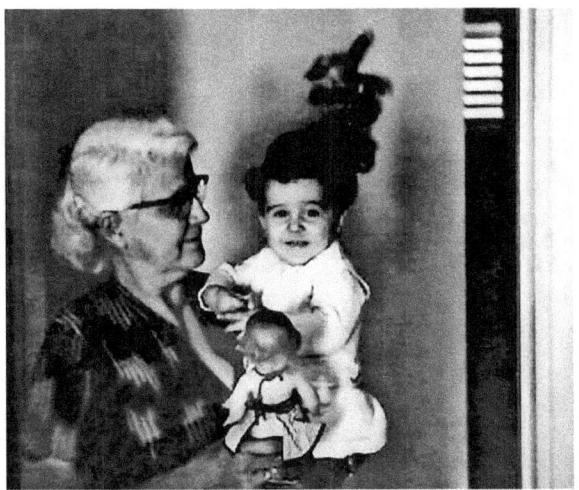

Turiana de la Torre, Vivian's paternal grandmother. Havana, Cuba, 1954.

I grew up with my brother, Alejandro, in our Santa Ana home in the Nuevo Vedado neighborhood of Havana. Alejandro was two years older than me. Surrounded by the simplicity and well-being our parents and grandparents cultivated, in addition to the warmth and affection they showered upon us, I had a life full of happiness.

Those wonderful years of my childhood were free of fear. I only remember how enthusiastic I was about riding my bicycle. My mind recalls the magical scene at the moment when I found it hidden in my grandparents' closet, spoiling the surprise my parents had prepared for me for Three Kings' Day.

My grandfather, Manuel, with his infinite kindness and boundless joy, became the most important

Vivian and her mother. Havana, Cuba, 1955.

person of my childhood. He was my closest ally and my greatest accomplice. As I sat on his lap, he would not only teach me how to turn the car's steering wheel but also how to place the domino pieces during animated evenings with his friends.

My grandfather taught me how to ride a bicycle and savor fruits, and I still treasure the hours spent with him as the most endearing moments of that golden time. That is why it pained me so much to leave my grandparents when we had to abandon Cuba in exile. I left part of my soul behind.

I turned five as Cuba was under a cloud of unrest and political turmoil. Fulgencio Batista's government was strongly criticized as corrupt, which led guerrilla forces to overthrow him. At 3:00 a.m. on January 1,

Vivian's first birthday celebration with her brother, Alejandro, and her parents. Havana, Cuba, 1955.

1959, Batista fled Cuba in a plane bound for Santo Domingo in the wake of the triumph of the Cuban Revolution led by Fidel Castro. At first, Batista remained in exile in the Dominican Republic, then on the island of Madeira (Portugal), and again in Marbella, Spain, until a heart attack took his life in 1973.

Unaware of what was going on, I could feel the anguish of my parents and grandparents. Their distress was not in vain. The news of the victors proclaiming their triumph and vowing vengeance against their defeated enemies was alarming. To some, the word "socialism" became synonymous with chaos, terror, and death, while to others, it meant freedom and justice. The illegal confiscation of the private assets of all citizens was the act of duplicity that, as Cubans

Vivian at her birthday party with family and friends. Havana, Cuba, 1959.

put it, "capped the bottle" and brought an end to hope. Life and freedom as we knew it had been "confiscated." The exodus and the division of Cuban families had begun. It was an absolute nightmare. Suddenly, everything was lost all at once. The dreams my grandparents had fulfilled disappeared from dusk to dawn. Everyone wondered, *Why? What did we do to deserve this? Who did we harm?*

In those days, my greatest act of independence was being able to ride my bicycle through the streets near my home or when I escaped to the Chinese cemetery, which was somewhat more secluded. But I clearly remember that afternoon when I was riding around the block, and suddenly, a big white car pulling out from one of the mansions brought me to a halt.

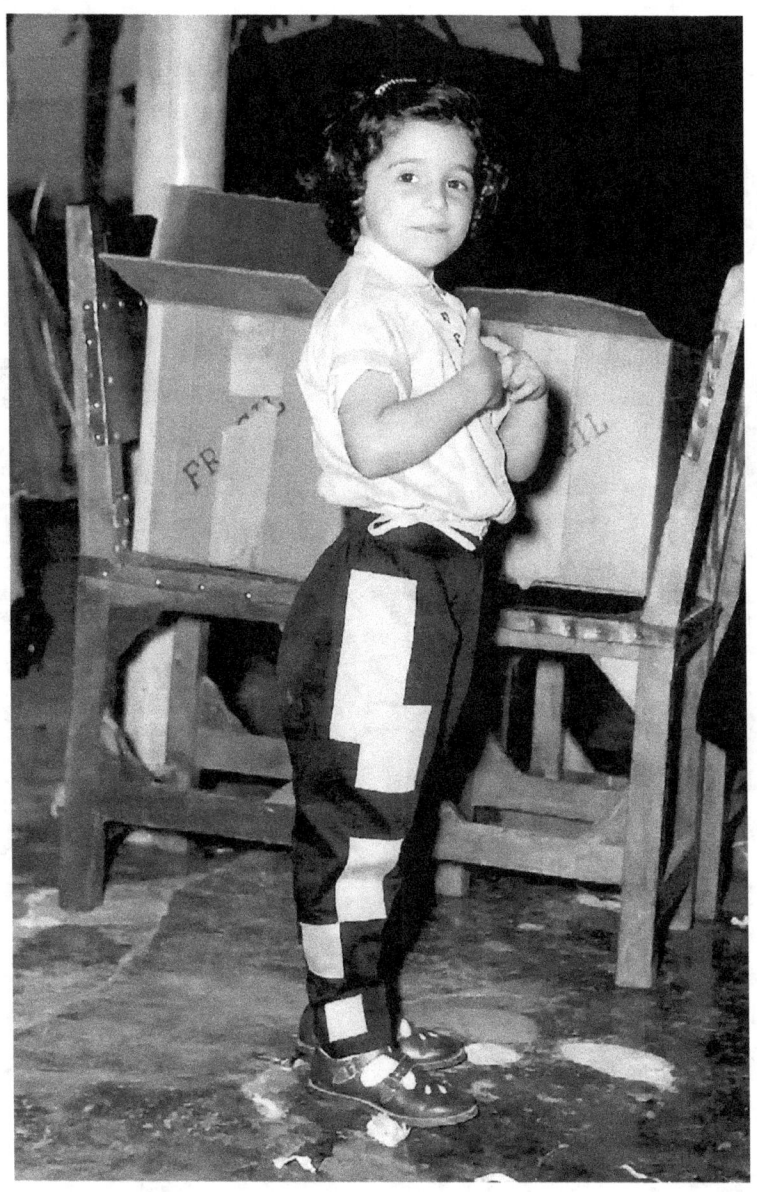

Vivian at the age of five at her birthday party.
Havana, Cuba, 1959.

Vivian at the age of five. Havana, Cuba, 1959.

THE CUBA OF MY CHILDHOOD

To my surprise, the passengers were Che Guevara and Camilo Cienfuegos. I watched them with fear, and right at that moment, they gave me an intimidating look. They both had a haughty attitude. I recognized them immediately since they were already famous. As a matter of fact, I was very attracted to Camilo Cienfuegos. The terror of such an encounter kicked in and made me speed off on my bicycle.

By that time, the Cuban Revolution had already started. Sometime after that episode, Camilo Cienfuegos suddenly "disappeared."

My dad, along with many other Cubans, was reluctant to believe what they saw with their own eyes. With a group of friends and a full understanding of the value of freedom, he went on a quest to protest the abuses, joining the Revolutionary Movement of November 30, created in 1960. This was the only movement my father was involved in throughout his entire life. His participation was limited to acts of political protest. He said that *he had always been a great individualist with an absolute fear of collectivities.*

He inherited his entrepreneurial spirit from my grandfather, Manuel, who, with his remarkable skill and vision, went from being a salesman to a sales manager at "Café Pilón." He would then become a vice president of the company and after that, a partner.

Café Pilón became the most famous brand of coffee in Cuba and the United States. The business exported coffee from Havana to Miami. Thousands of Cubans still remember its advertising slogan. My grandfather was an expert at extolling that catchy commercial Celia Cruz would sing as part of her performance during the splendor of Cuban television: "Café Pilón, tasty to the last sip."

The truth is that the Cuba we knew, the one my grandparents believed was the promised land as their destination after leaving their Spanish hometowns of Gijón and Bilbao, filled with dreams, would change forever.

What we were experiencing was just the beginning. The worst was yet to come.

CHAPTER 2

José Fernández de la Torre, Vivian's father; Lydia García, Vivian's mother; and Carlos Hüeck, at El Tropicana nightclub. Havana, Cuba, ca. 1957.

My First Farewell

In that faraway and painful month of April 1961, the sepulchral silence of two in the morning was shattered by the brutal arrival of the G2 to our home. Heavily armed men from that military intelligence group violently broke into our home after kicking down our door. They destroyed everything in their path. Their shouts and insults even woke up our neighbors.

I was sleeping in a room with Alejandro. I was seven years old, and my brother was nine. Out of despair, Mom ran to find us in our room, but she collided with the militiamen, who were armed with

Vivian's parents with her brother Alejandro. Havana, Cuba. 1952.

rifles and pistols. She was pushed out of the room. They searched the kitchen and took everything edible.

They found my father in the other room. I fearfully followed them with my eyes. I saw them grab him as he tried to throw on the first at hand after hearing the racket of the banging and pounding. My mother, disconcerted and unable to contain her cries, fired questions at the intruders and pleaded for them to take her as well. In response, those threatening beasts glared at her in hatred, provoking more tears, anguish, and impotence. Those were moments of terror.

My shocked grandparents could not comprehend the reason for such violence. Alejandro and I watched as my dad was handcuffed and shoved into a truck that would take him to an unknown destination.

At dawn, the search for my father became an ongoing pilgrimage to all the jails in Havana. And for weeks, my mother wandered through the streets with food and clothes she would leave under his name. However, he never received anything.

Like many other men and women who inquired after their relatives, never suspecting that all the cinemas, theaters, and stadiums had become prisons holding thousands upon thousands of Cubans, she relentlessly continued her interminable search for days. I would watch her in silence as she went out into the streets. My grandparents made a great effort to shield us from this. The same scene continued to replay for several months.

Her face was sunburnt from the merciless rays that beat down on her day after day on her exhausting and futile quest; finally, one day, she found him at the Blanquita Theater (today known as the Carlos Marx Theater). I was holding onto Mom's hand when I saw him from the street as he poked his head, with difficulty, through a small window. In one of life's great ironies, the same theater they had attended before as spectators had become my dad's prison. Then Senator of the Republic, Alfredo Hornedo Suárez, built that theater—the largest in the world at that time—and named it to honor his wife, Blanquita.

Now, the performance was being given by hundreds of militiamen who, from the enormous

Vivian with her mother and cousins at the Malecon walkway. Havana, Cuba. 1961.

stage, were pointing their rifles at the more than ten thousand prisoners, including both men and women, who were sitting in the theater's beautiful seats or standing on the lavish carpets. These captives were astonished as they observed the new characters of the Revolution, holding at bay big ferocious dogs, complementing their custodial mission. My mother was never permitted to see my father during the sixty days of his captivity in the theater.

Hungry, packed together, claustrophobic, and desperate with the heat and thirst, they protested for better treatment, the release of pregnant women who gave birth to their children in any available seat, and for the opening of the bathrooms since all the prisoners were allowed to use only one. To make their extreme distress more emphatic, men and women removed their shirts and confronted the militiamen, demanding their requests be met. However, they didn't succeed.

Instead, all they got in return were bullets, which led to the death of many of them, and the opening of small windows at the top of the theater to allow them to breathe.

Our home was overflowing with loneliness and sorrow. This tragedy deeply wounded the entire family and significantly impacted my childhood. Nevertheless, no one faltered. I believe love kept us united and strong. Thank God my mom wasn't taken away at that time. My dad was imprisoned after the invasion of the Bay of Pigs. That was unquestionably the first traumatic experience of my life.

Today, I remember everything with absolute clarity. My memory insists on evoking all of this. Years later, I would visit the island of Cuba and the neighborhood where I grew up. I would feel the music resonate within me in a different way, strengthening these roots. Something about those people, that land, and that sea made me feel complete.

One day, a few months later, my dad appeared at the door of our home. He returned pale, emaciated, extremely thin, and with a long beard. He was almost unrecognizable. Our joy was absolute, but it was only the preamble for a new separation.

After his release, Dad decided we had to leave Cuba, which, in addition to being prohibited by Fidel

Castro's government, was almost unfathomable. Making the official request took forever, and obtaining permission to leave could take nine, ten, or more years. Besides, we knew we'd never get a permit to leave!

So, my father decided to write letters to three friends in Venezuela, Panama, and Nicaragua. Weeks later, he received an answer from his great friend, Carlos Hüeck, President of the Beer Factory of Nicaragua, who sent a warm and positive response to my father's request to travel to Managua. He was the person who acted as the intermediary in processing the visas and permits with the Consul of Nicaragua in the Netherlands back then: Marcelo Ulvert, along with Guillermo Sevilla Sacasa.

Dad had to be present at the Rancho Boyeros Airport in Havana for ten days and wait for a seat on a KLM flight. Each day, we said goodbye to him until he was able to take the seat of a man who was removed from the plane for some random excuse. My father got through the red tape and managed to leave Cuba with the ticket Mr. Hüeck had sent to him.

The farewell at the airport was one of the hardest moments I had ever experienced emotionally. A deep pain tightened my chest so much I thought it would explode, and the discomfort made me vomit. I was filled with fear. After a long goodbye, with tears in his eyes, my dad walked up the stairs to board the plane. He quickly flashed a shadow of a timid smile and lifted his hand to wave goodbye.

MY FIRST FAREWELL

He left Cuba on a KLM plane on June 9, 1961, in search of a better future for him and us. He was still hoping to find it despite the uncertainty.

He left with his pockets empty, and his only luggage was his passport. He flew from Havana to Kingston, Jamaica, the only route to Miami. Once there, he had to sleep on a park bench.

Then, he had to wait until the next day to withdraw the money his friend Carlos Hüeck had sent him from the Royal Bank of Canada. He waited for a week before he received the authorization for his transit visa in Miami and then had to do the same to travel to Nicaragua.

When Dad finally arrived in Managua, Carlos Hüeck was waiting for him at the airport, and he uttered the phrase that would change the course of our lives: "Pepe, don't worry. As long as I am alive, you and your family will have everything you need." A hug sealed the affection and gratitude my dad would feel and express to him throughout his life. Don Carlos was like a father to him and, undeniably, a true angel.

Almost two months later, at the end of July 1961, my mother, my brother, and I were able to leave Cuba. We also traveled by KLM via Jamaica to Miami. We left the country penniless, with only a change of clothes in a small suitcase. That was all we could take from the island. We waited at the airport until four in the morning and finally managed to leave at ten in the evening, but the anxiety we felt the whole day was indescribable.

Everything on that long day was pure anguish. The feeling that pervaded those endless hours was uncertainty, and the thought you may never see your relatives again crushes your soul. Behind the glass, my grandparents' eyes were obscured by their tears as they anticipated the final goodbye.

I can still remember the strident voice of the security guard who called over the loudspeaker the names of the passengers whose departure from Cuba was arbitrarily canceled. My mother, nervous and afraid of the horror imposed by the "system," prayed that our names would not be the next to be called out.

Nevertheless, I felt the greatest fear when they inspected us. They first searched my mom, patting down her whole body. The officials were constantly monitoring people to make sure they didn't take any jewelry or money with them. After that, they exhaustively searched our very scanty luggage. I remember the angry scowl on the militiamen's face and their unconcealed contempt.

I felt like I was going to faint at inspection time because my mom had sewn into my pink fisherman pants her solitaire diamond ring, the one my dad gave her as an engagement ring. She didn't want to leave it behind, thinking she could sell it if needed.

The military official put his hand inside my pants, and I, who had seen my mother hide it there, felt the blood run down to my feet. It was a desperate act on my mother's part that could have cost us our exit from Cuba. I was still a child, and I don't know how

I managed to remain calm. Luckily for all of us, the man didn't discover the ring.

This method of hiding jewelry became common during the early days of the exodus. Our address and phone book of our friends and family in Miami was confiscated from my mother. We no longer had anyone to go to or to call if we got lost.

Once we were on board, the crew started calling the names of some people to get off the airplane. Terror was in the air. The plane reached the end of the runway, but the control tower gave the order to return. Everyone was trembling, thinking any one of us could be removed from the plane. My mother's face was filled with panic.

Finally, we departed for Jamaica. My mom was crying as she felt a jumble of nostalgia, anxiety, and joy. My grandparents and my cousins were in my mind, and curiously, I felt sad about leaving my bicycle.

I was leaving behind a happy life.

We arrived in Kingston after a 45-minute flight. Nobody said a word on the way. Emotions were mixed because we felt free but very afraid. We arrived at the hotel Carlos Hüeck had reserved for us. When we entered the hotel, we were warned not to leave because a strangler was on the loose.

So, my mother added another anguish to her already considerable worries. Once we entered the room, she closed all the windows and locked the door. We didn't leave that room at all during our stay.

The dolls that Vivian left in Cuba. Havana, Cuba, 1963.

Another reason we stayed inside was that the money my father sent us with his friend arrived, so we didn't even have enough money to eat! Carlos Hüeck had to send us some.

Two days later, we left for Daytona Beach, then Miami, and finally Nicaragua.

Once we arrived in Managua, we were able to hug Dad again, who was happily waiting for us at the airport.

This was a goodbye to our life in Cuba, to our grandparents, and to everything I knew up to that time. Finding a future in another land that opened its doors to us would be the next step.

CHAPTER 3

Vivian at the age of seven riding "Corsario."
Managua, Nicaragua, 1962.

Nicaragua: A New Beginning

On August 3, 1961, we arrived in Nicaragua. At the age of seven, I was disconcerted. I deeply missed my grandparents as well as the life I had in Cuba. There was a flood of emotions within me. Now, I knew what deep fear and desolation meant. For only a moment, the reunion with my dad allowed me to forget the mourning I was experiencing from the painful separation from my family. A new path was opening up before my eyes.

With Carlos Hüeck's help, my father started his new job in Nicaragua at Aceitera Corona, an oil-producing company. With the first payments he received, he was able to rent a space to live in the Colonia Molina area, on the fourth mile (at kilometer 6.5) of the southern highway. That place would be my refuge in Nicaragua.

Colonia Molina was on the outskirts of Managua, with Cerro Motastepe in the background. We were surrounded by vegetation. The properties in that area were still a far cry from the hustle and bustle of the cities, which were overrun with urban developments. This calming atmosphere helped me cope with my heartache.

Little by little, I discovered another world, nature, which taught me a new form of freedom. My companions were the trees, the rocks, the mountains, the cows, and above all: the horses. I entered the paddocks to herd them. I also rode bareback, jumping from a wall to get on the horse and riding through the countryside, making it gallop and stand up on two legs, holding onto its mane.

If I fell, I would immediately get up, act tough, and not cry over the spill. I would just dust off my rubber slippers and get back on. I didn't have time for anything else, not even to eat. I loved to bathe the horses, especially my mare Criolla, who had a white spot on her forehead.

I would give her bran and comb her mane. Life started to be beautiful again. I remember that every morning, Don Silverio, the owner of the horses we also rented for riding, would sell us a *pichinga*[1] with fresh cow's milk.

---

1 *Pichinga:* Container to transport milk and liquids.

NICARAGUA: A NEW BEGINNING

Vivian and her dog, León. Managua, Nicaragua, 1962.

I had a lot of contact with the people who lived near our house. They were humble people, good people, village people. I learned to drive a Jeep and would drive it around the cows, going up and down the mountain.

I preferred baseball instead of playing with dolls and played with my brother and his friends. Pitching to and playing tag with them fascinated me. I always liked exciting games, challenges, and unusual situations. I would climb the nearby *chilamate* trees. I had fun playing with the shooter marble and the *chibolas*.[2]

---

2 *Chibolas:* marbles, glass balls.—Ed.

My mother insisted on dressing me up like a girl, but I liked shorts for biking and horseback riding, climbing trees, and jumping fences. To me, dresses were "itchy."

The memories of my grandparents repeatedly flooded my memory. I conjured them up in my dreams. I wrote everything I dreamed of in the letters I sent to Cuba, and they answered me. Through their letters, they suggested names for our horses: Alejandro's horse would be named "Furia" and my mare, "Criolla."

It took up to six long months for the letters to get to Cuba. It was the only means of communication available because telephone calls had to be requested, and the government would grant them only when they wanted to. It could take two or three months for the Cuban regime to give this permission, and we were allowed to talk for only a minute since they would cut the call off all of a sudden.

The isolation at that time was total. Not only did I lose my grandparents, but I also lost my uncles, aunts, cousins, and godparents. There was no internet or cell phones. The world was different. The revolution in Cuba was worse than any revolution in Latin America. There, families were torn apart, and I was left without the rest of my family.

**

Private schools in Nicaragua were half a school year away and did not accept new students in the

Vivian at the age of eight, with her parents and her brother. Managua, Nicaragua, 1962.

middle of the term. That meant total freedom for me! At that stage, I matured a lot, maybe because I never fully assimilated the separation from my grandparents. I wrote them letters asking why we could not be together, and at the same time, I nourished their hope and mine by assuring them that in a not-too-distant future, we would meet again.

During that time, I had my first communion. I was extremely serious during the entire ceremony. I didn't smile for the photos since I was a shy girl who didn't like to be photographed. After the mass, we went to a restaurant to have breakfast with my parents and some friends. They took the usual photos, and my face was always a little bit sad. That's a great contrast to my life today, where laughter comes easily.

I started school soon after, but this transcendent event did not change my habits and character. I left Cuba after completing first grade and being the "excellence of the class," as we used to say in Cuba. Nevertheless, I was re-enrolled in kindergarten and first grade at the Colegio Americano Nicaragüense, the American school in Managua, because I did not speak English. The directors wanted to move me up to fourth grade, but I was afraid of changes. Certainly, leaving my loved ones and my home behind to move to a new country, especially in such a violent way, was part of my childhood trauma.

The Teresiano School was the solution to educate me because the nuns would apply more discipline. For the third time, and due to the different systems of the three schools, I had to attend first grade—another change, another regression, another way of seeing life that came to affect my character.

The strict regime suffocated me. My need for freedom clashed with the severity of the school. However, today, I think it was the best education I could have received.

I was enrolled in a semi-boarding school, taking classes from 7:00 a.m. to 5:00 p.m. and arriving home at almost 7:00 p.m. since the school was on the outskirts of Managua. I was the last one on the school bus route. During lunch, they served beans with weevils! Obviously, I put them aside so I could eat, but many times, some nuns forced me to swallow them. I would hide them in my uniform bag and show them to my mom when I got home.

Mother Valeria taught one of the classes. She used to say I had a call from God to become a nun. When she gave the class, she would look at me and raise her eyebrow. As we lined up for recess, she would ask me if I had already felt God's call. It gave me goosebumps! I was in sixth grade at that age, so I did not understand the significance of this vocation, but I felt the urgency of Mother Valeria to fulfill her mission to get more followers for her congregation. This situation frightened me so much that it added pressure and a new fear to my life. It was clear to me I did not want to become a nun, but Mother Valeria believed that, like her, I was "feeling that divine call."

I have always had enormous faith. God has been my island and my refuge. However, Mother Valeria's obsession affected me. My grades dropped, and that pressure disconcerted me, making me feel very insecure.

My mom was completely devoted to us. She was always happy and never complained about anything. Everything she did was for her happiness and that of others. The only thing that worried her was the burden of loneliness my grandparents had been left with.

Every time a letter arrived from Cuba, we celebrated because it brought news of our beloved homeland. We would sit around and listen as it was read aloud, laughing and crying.

In 1968, my grandparents, Manuel and Isidora, left Cuba via Mexico to come live with us in Nicaragua. My dad traveled to Mexico City to receive them. All I needed now were my other grandparents, Pachín and Turiana, and to recover from the time I lived without the special love and tenderness only grandparents can give.

I left them when I was 7 years old, and I saw them again when I was 14. The reception at the airport in Managua was unforgettable. I hugged and kissed them. Seeing them there seemed unreal. They couldn't stop talking and laughing. That reunion revitalized my life. I recovered part of my family. They came to live in our home and were immensely happy with us. However, one day, Mom told me: "Vivian, it's better not to move older people because they are used to their lives."

Soon, we heard about my grandfather Pachin's death on the island. My grandmother Turiana endured a year of solitude before traveling to Nicaragua in 1969. She moved into our house when I turned fifteen.

We moved to Bolonia, a more central location in the city of Managua. We were there until we built the house in the same neighborhood where we had lived for five years.

When I turned sixteen, I told my parents I wanted to change schools. I wanted to go back to the American school, and they agreed to it. This made me very happy, and it was a good decision. I attended classes from 7:00 a.m. to 12:00 p.m., drove my car

*Vivian on the day of her first communion.
Managua, Nicaragua, 1963.*

Vivian at the age of eleven. Managua, Nicaragua, 1965.

to get there, and made other friends who were more open-minded.

There, I met my great friend, Rogelia. I finished learning English and graduated. In the meantime, Dad had started his own company: Distribuidora Interamericana S.A. – DIASA, the largest food distributor in the 1970s in Central America.

I really enjoyed my teenage years and lived unforgettable moments with my friends. Every day was an exciting adventure. I was assigned the task of faking the written excuses our parents supposedly sent to justify our absences from school.

I had a special skill in mastering different handwriting styles and copying our mothers' signatures. There were so many fake messages that we were discovered and sent one by one to the principal's office because there were just too many coincidences. We sat down face to face with the principal, who kicked up a fuss and threatened to call our mothers. We were suspended for three days.

Immediately after, Rogelia called her house to warn Chepona, a domestic servant who loved her very much, spoiled her, and did everything she asked her to do so that she would pretend to be her mother when the school called. This woman went straight into imitating Rogelia's mother's voice.

The school principal, still not satisfied with Chepona's explanations, asked my mother to meet with her. Since my mother didn't speak English, I served as her translator, taking advantage of the situation to say the opposite of what the principal was telling me.

For example, the principal would say, "Lydia, your daughter doesn't pay attention in class," and I would translate for my mom, saying the principal had affirmed I was an excellent student. The principal would continue to list her complaints: "Lydia, your daughter is late for class," and I would say, "Mom, don't listen to this lady ... she is a little crazy," and I would tell the principal my mother assured me she would keep me in line from now on.

That scene would have made anybody laugh. In the end, my poor mother just nodded her head, and the director was satisfied. Later, I told my mom the truth about the principal's speech, and she answered me in her very Cuban accent, "Oh, for your mother's sake, Vivian, don't do this to me," and we laughed together.

When we weren't celebrating birthdays at any of our homes, we would go to the Drive Inn across from the old El Retiro Hospital to have some soft drinks.

That was where I first saw Carlos Pellas. I had no idea what destiny had in store for me.

CHAPTER 4

Vivian and her husband, Carlos. Miami, Florida, 1977.

Carlos Pellas: My Destiny

When you cross paths with someone, you never imagine how long they will remain in your life or what role they will play in it, much less which part of the path they will walk with you.

The day I met Carlos, I was with my friends, Maria Enriqueta, Rogelia, Mariel, and my brother. Carlos and Mike Wood, his best friend and partner from Stanford University, were at another table. Carlos called Ernesto, who was at another table, not knowing he was my ex-boyfriend, to ask if he knew me. He repeated my name several times since he had never heard it before.

*Vivian and Carlos at Lake Xiloa Lagoon.
Managua, Nicaragua, 1972.*

At that moment, I heard them spelling out "V-i-v-i-a-n" and commenting, "The Cuban girl this, the Cuban girl that … " Then I saw him wink at me as he walked by as a flirtatious sign. He kept inquiring about me. Some people told him they were going to introduce us. I got his name through Mariel and also found out we lived very close to each other.

There was no need for such an introduction. Carlos came to my house the day after he saw me at the Drive Inn. He knocked on the door, and my grandmother answered. He immediately asked to see me. She told him I was not there. Then, when I got home, she said, "Vivian, a boy came looking for you. He was wearing a Spanish beret. He is very handsome!"

Vivian on her graduation day. Managua, Nicaragua, 1974.

Carlos came back later. He found me sitting on the floor at the entrance to my home. He asked me on a date, but I told him I couldn't go. Up to that time, I had never been allowed to go out alone with a male friend, despite the fact I was seventeen years old and several young men were courting me.

So, a few days went by, until one day Carlos came back and said to me: "Well, you're like a lawyer: if you don't win, you confuse the case."

But since I liked him, I decided to ask permission to go out with him, and I got it . . . on the condition that a "chaperone" went with me!

Carlos mesmerized me from the moment I saw him. He was open-minded and different from everyone I had ever known. I was still quite young, but from that point on, he changed my life. My grandmothers adored him. He has always been a person of contrasts, outgoing, and open to the world. He had had many girlfriends, but his relationships didn't last long with any of them.

He says when he first saw me, he was struck by my eyes and felt as if life was coursing through his body when he looked at me. In fact, when we met, he would just stare at me. Later on, he told me the sensation he felt was like a kick in the chest and that his heart sped up until it felt like it was racing. There is no doubt: I married the love of my life.

It was 1971. Carlos was eighteen, and I was seventeen. We lived in the splendor of old Managua, a developing city with an identity, deep-rooted customs, and picturesque spots. Being steeped in that Managua was beautiful.

From his childhood, Carlos's life unfolded in a family environment. He lived in the San Dionisio coffee farmhouse with his three siblings, Alfredo, Silvio, and Lucia, and his twelve first cousins.

His family's origins go back to the days when his great-grandfather, Francisco Alfredo Pellas, a Genoese merchant, facilitated commercial navigation on Lake Cocibolca by acquiring and operating the Victoria Steamboat, a legend in the country's history.

Francisco Alfredo Pellas invested in the historic and renowned Compañía del Tránsito. Then, in 1890, he founded Nicaragua Sugar State Ltd., a company that recently celebrated its 129th anniversary.

Carlos's life in the countryside vanished when he moved to Managua to attend fourth grade at the Instituto Pedagógico. His father, Alfredo Pellas, saw the need for his children to start another way of life and to cultivate other relationships. Carlos completed his first year of high school at the Jesuit Centroamérica de Granada School and then transferred to a high school in northern California, the Woodside Priory School, where he completed this stage of his education.

He then enrolled at Stanford University in California to pursue a degree in Economics but not before taking his first steps in Engineering. That was his father's career, and he wanted Carlos to pursue it as well, forgetting about the skills test Carlos took at the Centroamérica de Granada School at the end of elementary school, where his great business skills were discovered. His father learned this when he received a note from the Jesuits explaining why Carlos should pursue a career in Administration, Economics, and Finance. The summer we met, Carlos was on a vacation in Managua. He has always said that, ever since he saw me at the drive-in, he thought: *This is the woman of my life.*

My brother, Alejandro, was no stranger to anything that was happening to me. He was always extremely jealous and protective. He frightened off all the young men who pursued me. He would pull me out of parties and take me home. The last time he did this to me was before the earthquake. He embarrassed me

Vivian at the age of seventeen. Managua, Nicaragua, 1972.

Vivian's thoughts recorded in the Colegio Americano Nicaraguense's Yearbook. Managua, Nicaragua, 1974.

so much that when we got home, I hit him with a shoe. After a few days, we forgot all about it.

My brother graduated in 1970. Sometime later, he moved to Miami, where he got married and had two daughters: Vanessa and Yamilee. My brother's absence from the family always hit us hard. We were extremely close. Forced separation has marked my family all my life.

I must have exchanged those nostalgic moments for my desire to grow and develop as a person. I graduated from high school with a degree in Bilingual Secretary.

My desire to work waned as long as my father clung to his philosophy that I didn't need to work as long as he did since I would never want for anything.

All my friends were working and began to develop as professionals. But he, with his overprotective mentality, thought it was enough that I had studied. However, I wanted more. I realized that dependency was not conducive to anything.

My dad was a noble man, a gentleman, brilliant, and endowed with a tremendous ability to persevere in life as a great professional and human being, just as he demonstrated throughout his career, overcoming all sorts of adversities.

I accompanied my mom to the supermarket and everywhere else. I loved to spend time with her. We enjoyed being together, we laughed a lot, and it felt as if I was spending time with a girl my own age. She had a great sense of humor, and that's essential in life. In short, I was her driver.

However, I had many aspirations, and those were reflected in my yearbook back then. My answer to the following question was written under my photograph:

What do you want to do in life?
"I want to be happy and try to make others happy."

I expressed what I was feeling. I didn't say things at random or just because I had to say something. Perhaps at that moment, even though I was still a teenager, the strength and desire to help the less fortunate were manifesting in me.

CHAPTER 5

El Plaza nightclub. Managua, Nicaragua, 1972.

Earthquake in Managua: 6.3 on the Richter Scale

All of a sudden, the earth awakened. In a fraction of a second, the old downtown center of Managua collapsed. An immense red trail took over the sky. The premonitions of superstitious grandmothers who smelled disaster were fulfilled. The clock of the old cathedral came to a stop when the calamity struck.

The catastrophe crept silently into the night. While nightlife was just starting for some, it was slumber time for others. The illusion of Christmas vanished. People woke up surrounded by debris and

Remains of a building in Managua after the earthquake. Managua, Nicaragua, 1972.

were forced to walk on it. The radiance of the beautiful capital was eclipsed as *taquezal*, adobe, and concrete buildings were left in ruins.

Shortly after midnight at 12:35 on December 23, 1972, Managua succumbed to an earthquake with a magnitude of 6.3 on the Richter Scale and two aftershocks. The earthquake was barely 3 miles deep. Nearly 20,000 people lost their lives. Only memories and destruction of our beloved Managua would remain.

That evening, Carlos, Alejandro, and I were at the El Plaza nightclub, the same one that collapsed an hour later! We had left there to go to a party. The earthquake sloshed the water in the pool as we stood around it. Carlos had to support me so I wouldn't fall

*Building in Managua after the earthquake.
Managua, Nicaragua, 1972.*

from all the cuts on my feet after walking on the broken glass of some large windows. We rushed to our homes, panicked, to make sure our families were alright.

On the way, Carlos told me we should go to my home first because his was built to withstand an earthquake of that magnitude, but there might have been some issues where I lived.

On the way, we saw huge gaping holes in the ground separated by deep fissures from the strong movement. Fortunately, everyone was safe, and my home was still standing, although it had some damage.

After that, Carlos ran to his house, and to his surprise and horror, his house had collapsed. A few seconds saved Lucía, his sister, since the movement of the earth woke her up before the wall of the room fell on her bed. His parents and brothers were miraculously alive as well. Carlos's parents were looking for Silvio, the youngest brother, because he couldn't be found. Carlos asked them to calm down because he wasn't home. He had snuck out that night. He was indeed out, partying. Carlos's house had to be completely rebuilt.

This was a terrible experience, especially for my parents and grandparents, because they never imagined an earthquake after all the adversity they had gone through. They were enjoying a party at a friend's house. Sometime later, my mother, with her best Cuban style, would say that after joyously dancing to the rhythm of an orchestra, they had to get out crawling on the floor.

In our house, the furniture and decorations were all out of place, glass was broken, and some minor cracks appeared in the walls. Because of the aftershocks, we had to sleep on the couch and some beds we brought out to the street for several weeks. DIASA, Father's company, was looted, as were all the buildings that were still standing.

Under these circumstances, my parents decided to send my grandparents to the United States because there were no hospitals, and their situation was becoming critical as elderly people in delicate health who could not stay with us.

Due to their condition, and with the assistance of some of my father's Guatemalan friends, a plane was sent to take them abroad. Alejandro returned to Missouri to continue his studies, and I stayed at home for a while until I went to study in Miami because no schools were standing in Managua. Once again, a separation.

The earthquake brought a new change to our lives, and Managua was never the same. The country's economic development was hindered, and Nicaragua regressed five years. Statistics reported 20,000 dead, 40,000 injured, and between 28,000 and 30,000 affected. The tragedy shocked the world. International aid mitigated part of the needs of the most vulnerable population, who lost everything. Little by little, these people came back with great effort to rebuild their lives and homes.

Once again, we were devastated by the tragedy and by the separation from our loved ones. My dad, with his ongoing entrepreneurial spirit, built a new home where we lived until 1979, when another story began for our family: the Sandinista Revolution.

CHAPTER 6

Vivian at Colegio Americano Nicaragüense at age seventeen. Managua, Nicaragua, 1971.

Changing Horizons

My life took a different path as I was determined to start my adult life on the right foot. Carlos insisted I had to study a career, and that was the push I needed. So, I went to Miami's Barry College in 1975, which was my choice after the earthquake crushed the American school floor to floor. Luckily, the earthquake happened after midnight. Otherwise, the death toll would have been considerably higher.

All my life, I have been an art lover, and that's why I decided to study Interior Decoration. I loved decorating, but that department was closed during my application process. Then, I decided to enroll in

Liberal Arts. I took classes in drawing and metal arts, as well as general classes in art history and painting techniques.

Dad visited me in Miami once and joined me in one of my university classes. As it so happens, right on that day, a male model attended the class in a bathrobe, which he took off with a flourish, leaving him as God sent him into this world before the astonished eyes of my father and me. I hadn't expected such an activity that day; otherwise, I wouldn't have had my dad come with me!

Upon his return, he indignantly told my mom, "How is it possible that your daughter is painting a naked man when the hardest thing to draw is the hand of a man? Why do they need to make her draw a naked man?"

I was deeply attached to my mom. Being separated from her caused immense heartache for both of us. I had spent a year at Barry College but had to give up my studies because Mom longed to see me so much and couldn't stand our separation. I had created a deep-seated dependency with her and decided to return to her side. We both needed each other.

However, this experience taught me that dependency is not good. Mom didn't drive, and I, who was her "driver," was always ready to take her to the shops. We both provided each other with a lot of companionship and spent our time very happily together. Those were beautiful moments!

I was admitted to Centro Americana University - UCA, the first private university in Central America. There, I studied humanities and history for three

*Vivian and Carlos at a costume party.
Granada, Nicaragua, 1973.*

years with great professors I remember with special admiration.

In the meantime, my relationship with Carlos continued. He was never a difficult man. He was never still; he was always on the go. He was lighthearted as well as tireless! However, he was dominant at times. The vision of what I wanted to do with my life was becoming stronger. I was not attracted to Carlos for his economic status. My love for him was greater than the ambition any woman could ever feel for a man of his standing.

The distance strengthened our love. The desire to see each other on every trip Carlos made to Nicaragua was increasingly stronger, and we felt the need to share our daily experiences. A couple of times, I went

Vivian and Carlos on the day of their engagement. Managua, Nicaragua, 1975.

to California to see Carlos without my parents knowing. I was traveling for the weekend, and I would stay with him for four days. When I returned, I would write him letters telling him about what I was doing in his absence.

Other times, when he came to Nicaragua and my father didn't give me permission to go out, I would sneak out the kitchen door with my mother's consent. When I had Dad's approval to go out, my mom would turn the clock hands back so I could enjoy a little more time with Carlos. They never gave me the keys to the house, and Mom always stayed awake, sitting on the living room couch, waiting for me.

Another way we found to communicate was the ham radio system. Carlos was a big fan of it. That system could support communities at risk during emergencies. For years, demonstrating skill in using Morse code was required to obtain a ham radio license. Carlos got his and would install it wherever he was. At the same time, making long-distance calls at that time was extremely expensive, so this little solution saved us a lot of money for five years!

In fact, our long-distance relationship worked quite well. I used the phone, and Carlos was on his radio. However, it wasn't easy to speak freely with this technology because I would say, for example, "Carlos, I love you very much, over and out," and anyone could hear the conversation. So, we had to develop a private code to achieve the desired communication. Mine was: "Two happy hearts," and his was: "Potato Charlie, a broken heart."

We planned to marry in September of the following year. Carlos had to finish his master's degree and, afterward, work for two months in a bank in the United States to gain more knowledge as a finance major. My mom and I spent that time preparing for the wedding.

After his two months of work at the bank were over, Carlos decided to return from San Francisco to Nicaragua by land. He did so in the company of his brother Alfredo. A trip that should have taken a week ended up taking a month and a half. I was upset because I wanted him to be with me to decide certain details of the wedding. He showed up in August with a big smile on his face, one month before the wedding, claiming this trip was his "bachelor's party."

During his last vacation in December 1975, he had given me the engagement ring at home, in front of my parents, my grandparents, and his parents.

My family was delighted. Their beloved daughter was getting married.

CHAPTER 7

*Vivian and Carlos on their wedding day.
Managua, Nicaragua, September 4, 1976.*

Happiness Knocks at My Door

Carlos came into my life to stay. Without realizing it, he became part of my very being. He was more than I could have ever imagined. He was my dream, but he also represented my longing for freedom. His presence filled me completely. His enormous intelligence and personality always captivated others, and I was no exception.

Love was also a form of independence. Carlos transmitted his confidence to me, and I started to have more confidence in myself. And with him, I learned to say "No" ... well, at least sometimes!

*Vivian and Carlos on their wedding day.
Managua, Nicaragua, 1976.*

The five years of our long-distance relationship ignited the flames of a love that has not yet been extinguished. I totally fell in love with him, with that pure and true love. He, as a person, filled my spaces.

My father taught us that people should be appreciated for their true value, meaning for what they were, and not for what they had. Without a doubt, in addition to the way my exile from Cuba marked me, that lesson put my feet on the ground. I could have had nothing, but my morale was always high in that regard. My parents related to people for what they were and not for what they had. I married Carlos for love.

To my parents, Carlos was a son who, to a large extent, filled the void my brother had left.

Vivian and Carlos on their wedding day at the Church of San Francisco. Managua, Nicaragua, 1976.

*Vivian and Carlos with their parents.
Managua, Nicaragua, 1976.*

My parents organized the wedding at the Church of San Francisco, and some details were agreed upon with Doña Nena, my mother-in-law. Carlos had chosen his godparents, and I had chosen mine. However, following protocol, our main godparents had to be President Anastasio Somoza and his wife, Doña Hope Portocarrero Debayle.

For Carlos's family, this was a bitter pill to swallow. This was particularly true for his father, Alfredo Pellas, since he was part of the opposition. My father had previously spoken to him to explain he had invited the president as a token of gratitude for the decent treatment he had given Cuban exiles. Alfredo Pellas, who was ever a gentleman, answered: "Pepe, whatever you want is fine."

Carlos Pellas and his father-in-law, José Fernández. Miami, Florida, 1982.

We enjoyed the party until 5:30 a.m., breaking the tradition of the bride and groom leaving the gathering at one in the morning. The next day, we flew to Miami, and two days later, we were off to Europe.

Our destination airport was Madrid and later Portugal by train, where we looked for the huge Volvo that Carlos's father had leased to buy in Lisbon. We used it during the month of our honeymoon travels, and after that, he sold it from Nicaragua at the same price he paid for it, like any good businessman. It was a very comfortable trip because we didn't have to move around in trains with the hassle of loading suitcases in terminals or using taxis everywhere we went. We traveled on a low budget and made the most of it.

We would spend three or four days in one place. If we got bored, we would go to another one. Everything was spectacular, but we were returning to our reality. It was an unforgettable trip. Our honeymoon filled us with the energy we needed to start a new life together.

Once back in Nicaragua, we stayed with my parents for fifteen days. Then, we rented a house, and after two years, we built our own, which is the same one we live in today: a small and comfortable home we have been enlarging. Living as a family in a house full of nostalgia and beautiful memories, surrounded by nature's bounty that brings us immense peace, is something we find fulfilling.

Finding Carlos in my life and walking hand in hand with him has been a blessing from God. He was already important to me back then, but he became even more so for all his presence meant to me in the events to come...

CHAPTER 8

Vivian and Carlos with Alfredo and Carmen Pellas, Carlos's parents. Managua, Nicaragua, 1975.

A New Life

I never imagined that, by getting married, I would be committed to an intense social life. Carlos had been assuming the management of some companies that would require him to maintain relationships with a variety of people in Nicaragua and abroad. I felt strange but nonetheless happy. However, I wondered if it would be this way for the rest of our lives.

At one of the many family reunions, one of Carlos's uncles commented: "Now Vivian and Carlos will represent the family and will have to attend all the social events." My answer was: "One moment, that's not why I got married. I'm very sorry, but my husband and I will decide which events we will attend." I never knew if he was joking about it, but my answer was categorical.

It is true I liked attending some social events, and I would do it gladly and with great pleasure. But everything has a limit. We were both clear that we wanted to preserve our independence. For that reason, we needed to have our own space.

Carlos's passion had always been fishing. It was his oxygen, his escape. It had always fulfilled him. At the same time, I would assume my individuality. When Carlos asked me to go fishing with him, I would refuse to go because that wasn't my hobby (plus I would get seasick). I would tell him that "I had already caught my great Marlin," referring to him. He would laugh at my answer.

Nonetheless, I never questioned my decision to get married. I left my home, and now I had greater independence. I was starting a stage of maturity. Marriage was opening a new path, and facing this new challenge enticed me. I loved my husband deeply, and I happily took on the challenge of married life.

A very important business trip for Carlos was the one he took to Cuba in 1977 when he was invited to the convention of Latin American and Caribbean Sugar Exporters (GEPLACEA). By accompanying my husband on this trip, I had the chance to return to the land of my parents, to relive my childhood experiences, and to see my old house and my old neighborhood. I was coming back with a different mindset, and my expectations were enormous.

Newlyweds Vivian and Carlos. Miami, Florida, 1977.

Carlos Pellas fishing.
San Juan del Sur, Nicaragua, 1978.

My dad didn't want me to take that trip because of the risk involved and the terror he felt. He thought they would detain me and prevent my departure from Cuba. I traveled with Carlos as a member of the Nicaraguan delegation. Fausto Amador, who managed Somoza's assets, went as well. Don Fausto intended to find and recover his grandson, the son of Carlos Fonseca Amador, founder of the Sandinista National Liberation Front, who had his son in Cuba. But the latter didn't want to return with Don Fausto.

We traveled with Nicaraguan passports. My father warned me not to talk in any room because there were microphones everywhere. He insisted I shouldn't say a word and that I should never leave Carlos's side because I could be *disappeared*. Nevertheless, I traveled with certain precautions.

Contrary to what everyone thought, the first visa authorization to arrive at the embassy was mine. I was excited about my return. My adrenaline was pumping at its peak. From the moment we arrived, I was immensely surprised because I had never been treated so well in a country.

Upon our arrival at the airport, I relived the traumatic moments of 1961 when my dad was escaping from Cuba. The protocol agents pulled me back to the new reality and gave me preferential treatment as if I had been the head of the delegation. We were transferred to the Free Havana Hotel, formerly known as the Havana Hilton, which was paradoxically built by the sugar workers of Caja del Retiro Azucarero de Cuba in 1952.

I received constant attention. I would get up in the morning and go downstairs to the lobby, where the person in charge of protocol stalked me with questions such as: "Mrs. Pellas, how are you doing? Are you happy? What do you want for breakfast? Do you want to do something extraordinary today?" Feeling uncomfortable with the excessive scrutiny, I rushed back up to my room and locked myself in.

I turned twenty-three on March 5 in Havana. I was alone in my room and did not attempt to leave while Carlos was working. He made a point of insisting I not open the door if I was alone and somebody knocked. He would also urge me not to speak because there were microphones behind the paintings and under the shoes. Furthermore, he would say that G2 (the secret police) might come after me for being Cuban.

On my birthday, Carlos was supposed to attend an important meeting during his convention. With fear on every inch of my skin, I heard someone knocking on the door, followed by absolute silence. *They are really coming for me!* I thought. Suddenly, I heard a voice outside saying:

"Mrs. Pellas?"

"Yes!"

"Open up, please!" "No, I can't."

"Look, we've got something for you!" "Leave it there."

"But it's something very special!"

"Leave it," I said emphatically, waiting for them to break the door down.

But I didn't open it. I didn't want to be taken away or disappear without being able to let Carlos know. Two hours later, someone knocked on the door again, and I said to myself, *Now they're really coming for me!* I asked:

"Who's there?"

"It's me!" I heard Carlos's voice.

When I opened the door, Carlos and I were surprised to see a huge bouquet of flowers with a card that said, "Happy Birthday," signed by Fidel Castro Ruz.

I hugged Carlos. Then I put the card away, and we went down to the hotel bar to celebrate my birthday amidst the uncertainty and fear that the idea of becoming the object of Fidel Castro's attention caused in me.

The sugar producer convention continued the next day. And despite my fears, I decided to take the risk of attempting to visit my former home, the one the regime confiscated from us.

CHAPTER

Vivian with her great aunt and great uncle. Havana, Cuba, 1977.

Reliving the Past

I arrived at my old home in Cuba accompanied by the Nicaraguan Ambassador to Belgium. I got out of the car and knocked on the door, but no one was there. I was told one of the men who was part of the attack on the presidential palace targeting Batista lived there and that the Cuban Regime had given him the house as a reward. Nevertheless, I couldn't get in. It was locked.

It was a beautiful house. I had lived in it for the first seven years of my life. I wanted to see what had survived after I left. My heart was beating with anguish and emotion as the memories of that early morning when my dad was arrested came flooding back.

I envisioned my room and my dolls and sighed for a few minutes. I looked through the windows and into the house. I needed to find clues to my life, my family, and my grandparents. Everything in that home filled me with nostalgia. I wanted to find traces of that time of happiness.

I walked around to the back of the house and saw the windows of my room. I could see the same furniture in the living room and the same TV. The gray granite floor where I played jacks with a small ball was intact. After that, I walked to the garage where I had kept my bicycle. It was gone.

I remembered how I was unable to get anything out of my home when I left the island. We left with a small suitcase that had only a change of clothes for each of us. I was carrying a pink shirt and fisherman pants of the same color, into which my mom had sewn the ring, and I was wearing the handmade lace and organza dress, a gift from my godmother, who had exquisite taste and always gave me the finest dresses made in Cuba.

It was a moment in a dream where I was transported to an almost unreal world . . . I was a character in my own story. I was detached from my reality and immersed in my dream world, rediscovering the emotions I felt in my old house. In my imagination, I walked through the house, perceiving each aroma and going through every room.

For a few moments, I stood completely still as I was lost in this reverie.

Suddenly, I opened my eyes and woke up, grateful for the precious moment I had experienced. The people who accompanied me were surprised. My heart was racing at a rate of millions of beats per second as I experienced the most beautiful of my memories and longed to go back to that time. My inner being was bursting with nostalgia and longing.

Some ladies who were friends of my grandparents lived across the street from the house. I crossed the street and knocked on the door. They opened it and asked who I was. I said I was "Isidora's granddaughter," and they immediately recognized me and said, "This is Vivian, the girl with the *colochos*."[3]

They opened the only bottle of liquor they owned and had saved for many years as a relic.

Encouraged to continue releasing my emotions, I asked the driver to take me to Old Havana to visit my great aunt, Josefa Rivera Humará. Shaking, I called her on the phone. It had been seventeen years since I last saw her!

"Hello, can I speak to my Aunt Josefa?" "Yes, I can hear you. Who is this?"

"It's Vivian."

"Vivian who?"

"Vivian Fernández, your niece."

"Do you mean Vivian Fernández?"

---

3 *Colochos:* Curls.

"Yes, this is Vivian Fernández."
"Don't joke with me, please."
"Auntie, I am Vivian."
"Oh my God, I can't believe God is opening the gates of heaven for me today!"

All these events were surreal. I felt emotions that are indescribable even to this day.

When I arrived, all the neighbors in the badly damaged building with unpainted walls were waiting for me in the street. I went up the stairs to the second floor of her apartment because, as she told me later, my aunt could not come down from all the anxiety she was feeling. She was trembling. She hugged me, we hugged each other, we cried, she kissed me, and I kissed her, she touched my hair, and she looked at me to make sure I was the same person she thought I was.

She asked about my grandmother Isidora, her beloved sister, her only sister. She also asked about my brother, her niece Lydia, my mother, her son José Antonio, who she called "Pepín," his wife, and her only grandson. She took me into her kitchen and showed me a pot of peas and said, sobbing: "Vivian, this is what they give us. I cook them for hours, and they never get soft. I have nothing to offer you."

Then, making sure no one could see her, and with a frightened look on her face, she took out some jewelry that belonged to my mother and her daughter-in-law she had been keeping. She gave me her daughter-in-law's wedding ring and a cross. There was a ring with an aquamarine stone that belonged to my mother, which she didn't want to give me, fearing that something would happen to me on the street in a country of terror where owning jewelry is a crime.

We went out to the balcony, and together we contemplated—still with tears in our eyes—the devastation of the landscape of Cuba's past, the crumbling buildings that seemed to say: *time has stopped here, leaving us abandoned for eternity.*

Carlos and I invited my aunt and her husband to the Moscú Restaurant. They hadn't tasted any of this food in more than fifteen years. They hadn't even had a sip of rum in all that time.

After that trip, the only contact I had with my aunt Josefa was through letters. She died a few years later in the presence of a neighborhood boy whom I had been able to meet during my furtive visit. She had grown fond of him as if he had been her grandson. The boy reminded her of her only son and her little grandchild, who were living outside of Cuba and whom she never saw again. I gave that little boy a piece of gum, and he was surprised because he didn't know what it was.

When I returned to the hotel, my Nicaraguan friends, who were also part of the delegation, asked how the visit with my aunt had gone. I didn't have the words to give them an answer. I had just gone through a shocking experience and began to weep in dismay. We returned to Managua, and I did not delay in telling my parents about all my experiences. They listened anxiously.

I had asked them to come with me, but they did not accept. They never wanted to return to Cuba. They had too much pain in their hearts. They loved their country deeply and preferred to keep the memory of their homeland of the past. Visiting the Cuba of today would affect them too much. They had already closed that chapter now that their friends and family surrounded them in their new homeland of Nicaragua.

CHAPTER 10

*Vivian when she was nine months pregnant.
Miami, Florida, 1979.*

The Exodus, a Ghost behind Us

Exile is such a strong experience that only those who have gone through it can understand it. But the exile we had back then was terribly cruel. First, you had to fight to get out, and then, if you succeeded, you knew that perhaps it would mean leaving your country, your family, your homeland ... forever.

After my visit to Cuba, my mom asked me to tell her in detail about my meeting with her aunt Josefa. When I told her about the ring with the aquamarine stone, she nostalgically told me she would have liked to keep it because it had been the gift her father had given her on her fifteenth birthday.

Carlos Francisco's baptism. Miami, Florida, 1979.

Those memories took my mom back to her youthful experiences in Havana and to the harsh experiences she had to go through when Castro's guerrillas stepped up their actions to overthrow Batista. Paradoxically, the same thing was happening in Nicaragua: the guerrillas of the Sandinista Front were expanding their actions against Somoza, and, of course, that filled her with great anxiety.

Mom had a friend who was a follower of esoteric beliefs and the unknown. One day, she accompanied that friend, Elsye Usategui, to one of those sessions with more skepticism than anything else, and at her insistence, she agreed to get a card reading. Each of the woman's sighs was an alert for my mother to say to herself, *What lie will she come up with now?*

Lydia Fernández, with her grandson Carlos Francisco. Managua, Nicaragua, 1980.

After many cards were drawn and revealed, the woman said, "I see you surrounded by buildings in another country," and my mother replied with that confidence that only she could have: "Look, lady, you're wrong because I'm an exile from Cuba and, even if communism comes here, I'm not leaving again."

The session ended with the respective wink of her friend, who, a little embarrassed, paid the bill, making a hasty retreat. Three years later, my mom was living in New Jersey because everything Dad owned had been confiscated in Nicaragua during the Revolution of 1979, and therefore, they actually did end up "surrounded by buildings in another country."

By 1979, the situation was becoming more dangerous every day. Any political activity triggered

Vivian and her children Carlos Francisco and Vivian Vanessa. Miami, Florida, 1982.

demonstrations and confrontations against Somoza's National Guard, which responded by throwing tear gas bombs or firing weapons to disperse the students. I decided to continue my education by enrolling in the Centro Americana University, the UCA.

When there were protests in the streets, a group of classmates and I hid in terror under the desks to avoid stray bullets. Once again, I had to abandon my intention of graduating with a college degree by leaving the country. I was seven months pregnant, and all I wanted was to hold my first child in my arms. I could not expose myself to a fatal accident. Once again, exodus was knocking at our family's door like a ghost lurking in the shadows, and this time due to another confrontation between brothers and sisters.

The happiness my first pregnancy brought to the entire family distanced us from the horrors of war for some time. We decided to travel to Miami to await the birth of Carlos Francisco. My in-laws allowed us to use an apartment on the beach they had recently purchased. The world revolved around the expectation of our first child. The grandmothers, the grandfather, my parents, and Carlos were with me. Our son was born on June 8, 1979, in Miami.

From the hospital bed, I followed on the TV the news about the war in Nicaragua.

Carlos Francisco was a restless boy, but he always had the advantage of so many arms to carry him. I tried to breastfeed him, but the anxiety that the news about Nicaragua provoked prevented me from producing enough milk to do so. My father had lost everything after eighteen years of hard work.

The situation around us was tense. Fortunately, my parents stayed on to provide us with support and company, which I found extremely helpful.

After a few months, my parents decided to move to New Jersey. The news from Managua was not encouraging. One of Dad's friends told him what was going on. He told my father not to even try to come back because they had started confiscating properties and sending people to prison was the norm.

My dad lost everything and no longer wanted to return to Nicaragua. He preferred to face exile. Again, he had to relive the tragedy of Cuba. But they stayed in the United States for only a year. They could never get used to living there. That was not the country they wanted for their future; they loved and were used to the Latin lifestyle.

Two months after Carlos Francisco's birth, my husband and his cousin, Alberto Chamorro, decided to travel to Nicaragua on a private plane to take control of the companies. As they flew over the city of León, they heard Commander "Zero" on the radio shouting at a Sandinista rally: "All those with blue and green eyes are going to be hung from a tree." Carlos has green eyes, and his cousin has blue eyes! The pilot looked at them and asked: "Are you sure you want to land in this country?" They decided to go ahead and face the situation despite the threat. They arrived in Managua without any problems. This visit was decisive for my return to Nicaragua with Carlos Francisco, who was barely three months old.

The day I traveled alone with my baby to Nicaragua, I carried water and food for him because of the food shortage the country was already experiencing. But the most discouraging reality of all was the hatred and anger in the eyes of the military. They proudly wore their red and black scarves around their necks. These scenes were intimidating, and we experienced them every two or three months since we did not want to leave the country despite the hard times we were going through. We had to live on both sides.

I remember the time when Carlos Francisco was two years old and got conjunctivitis. We had to ask some of his father's friends for help so we could get

Vivian and one-year-old Eduardo. Miami, Florida, 1987.

medicine for his treatment from Guatemala with the assistance of a flight attendant.

We made the most of our stay in Miami by doing everything we were unable to do in Nicaragua, including baptizing Carlos Francisco. My friend, Rogelia Urcuyo, was his godmother and Silvio Pellas, his godfather. Just hearing the news that the Sandinistas were going to "hang the bourgeois on the road to Masaya" filled us with panic and made us board a flight to Miami. There was so much instability we had to hire a tutor for Carlos Francisco to teach him second grade from our home.

In the midst of this chaos, Carlos did not want to disengage himself completely from his companies in Nicaragua. The multiple devaluations and fluctuations of the exchange rate made doing business impossible.

In the late 1980s, due to the government's stringent measures to dominate the entire political and economic spectrum, Carlos thought he was wasting his time in the country. The government was moving forward with sweeping economic controls, and in June 1988, it confiscated the San Antonio sugar mill, which was one of the country's and the family's main companies. The entire economic system was artificial, and the people were soon impoverished. The country's economy shrank dramatically. It was a total disaster. Society was producing nothing.

Carlos's involvement in all the work of the San Antonio sugar mill since he was thirteen years old allowed him to have a global vision of this great company. He learned everything from the ground up, from cutting and loading sugarcane to driving the tractors. He liked everything related to production: he assimilated every report from any department with extraordinary understanding.

He had to negotiate during the hard times of the Sandinista era with the men and women who were union members, with machine guns in hand or on the table, and pressure of all kinds. Carlos would tell them if they didn't take the machine guns off the table, there would be no negotiation.

The devaluation rate was 7% per week. There were no investments or foreign currency. People spent whatever they earned so their money would not depreciate. The time came when the devaluation was so critical, and the number of zeros on prices was so high that the official exchange rate of the Nicaraguan cordoba against the United States dollar was five million to one! Computers couldn't handle those figures, and budgets meant nothing. Money was better weighed than counted. Companies had to change all the accounting categories and work with unit systems: certain machine hours per day for so many man-hours of work. New codes were implemented. Inflation and devaluation set us back forty-five years, and the country became poverty-stricken.

Carlos started proposing new strategies, such as the expansion of business to Central and South America as well as to the United States. The travel commitments and demands increased. Our lives oscillated between two countries and two cities: Miami and Managua. We would try to take the children to Nicaragua for summer, Christmas, and Easter holidays.

Amidst this dizzying pace of life, Vivian Vanessa was born on March 20, 1982, in Mercy Hospital, and Eduardo was born on June 6, 1986, in South Miami Hospital. I was looking forward to the birth of a girl, but during my pregnancies, I never wanted to know the gender of my children. Vivian Vanessa and each of my children were a surprise that brought immense happiness.

The three of them were free spirits. Carlos Francisco won prizes in chess contests, Eduardo said he was going to join the major leagues, and Vivian Vanessa was excited about following my passion for dance. At this stage of our lives, I spent more time with my children in Miami, and Carlos did the most traveling.

The three of them developed a special relationship with their grandparents and great-grandparents, who made their grandchildren the center of their lives. My parents never failed my children, who, in turn, developed an unwavering love for their grandparents.

My parents had already settled in Honduras when Vivian Vanessa and Eduardo were born. I would take the children all the way there so my parents could look after them and enjoy their company. I always had the support of my parents, no matter how far away they were.

The situation in Nicaragua was extremely precarious due to the devastation the civil war wreaked upon the country from 1981 to 1989. This had a negative impact on the lives of all Nicaraguans, especially in terms of health and the economy. The U.S. government declared a blockade on the Nicaraguan government, and among other things, airlines were not allowed to fly directly from any U.S. airport to Nicaragua.

When I was three months pregnant with Eduardo in December 1985, I was still making constant trips back and forth between Miami and Nicaragua. On one occasion, I came down with a severe cough that five months later led to pneumonia, a torn pleura, and throbbing pain every time I coughed.

The doctor who treated me in Miami had to give me medication, warning me about the possibility of side effects that could put the baby's life at risk. But it was impossible to avoid taking it because the cough was giving me shortness of breath. When I took it, it produced labor-like pains that were unbearable. I had to go to my gynecologist, who immediately told me to lower the dose of the medicine I had been prescribed. Five months into the pregnancy, he ordered neurological tests to check the condition of the fetus.

The results were devastating. The doctor, Juan José Lugo, was clear and honest with me and Carlos when he gave us his diagnosis: spina bifida. Science recommended abortion.

At that moment, I felt my child turning over. Carlos, with an utterly somber look on his face, told me he would respect and support any decision I made. I understood I would even be putting the stability of my marriage at risk, but I never doubted I would have the baby.

It was a crucial moment and, unquestionably, one of the hardest and best decisions of my life. For the rest of my pregnancy, I prayed to God all the time for my child to be born without that malformation.

I will never forget the moment when Eduardo was born. The doctors started counting the parts of his body one by one ... and at the end, they gave a sign of

*Vivian's father with his three grandchildren.
Miami, Florida, 1987.*

good physical condition and confirmed that everything about him was normal! Everyone in the room applauded with excitement, including Carlos and Dr. Lugo, who is Eduardo's godfather today.

In 1986, we became more firmly established in Miami, even though I had a hard time adjusting to this new life. Sometimes, I cried because I was very lonely since Carlos had to travel every month. The reason was that Nicaragua had this famous law of absence, under which the Sandinista regime would confiscate all your goods if you spent more than six months out of the country.

When we decided to settle in Miami, my parents had already decided not to stay in New Jersey. They wanted to be closer to Nicaragua, their grandchildren,

Vivian tap dancing. Miami, Florida, 1991.

*Vivian and her best friend, Rogelia Urcuyo.
San Juan del Sur, Nicaragua, 1990.*

Carlos, and me. Therefore, they thought Honduras was the most appropriate country to relocate to and to start a third exile.

My parents and my in-laws were always with me for every birth, and fortunately, another angel accompanied me in my loneliness. Her name was Mina. At a very young age, she began working at a coffee shop in Hacienda San Dionisio in San Marcos.

In 1981, although I lived between Miami and Managua, I always maintained my relationship with my lifelong friend, Rogelia, the godmother of my son Carlos Francisco. I talked to her about my life. I felt the need to share all the realities of daily life. And who better to share them with than a good friend who has always been like a sister to me?

**

Something happened to me one day in 1987. I was going down a street near my home, on which I had already seen a dance studio. I would even walk by that place every morning, afternoon, and evening. I would look at it, but I never dared to go inside. On one occasion, I decided to take a closer look at the place, and I made it to the door. The owner, Ruth Michaels, mother of the famous choreographer Mia Michaels, came out and asked me if I was interested in dancing. That was all the impetus I needed.

Mia won an Emmy Award. She used to work as a choreographer for important companies and celebrities, such as Cirque du Soleil, Celine Dion, and Gloria Estefan, among others.

Since I was a little girl, dancing was one of my greatest dreamscapes. I remembered how my grandfather Manuel and my mother danced with natural ease, and that inspired me. I enrolled at Joe Michaels Dance Studio in Miami and decided to take tap dancing. That's how I got involved in dance. I performed for the first time in the Miami-Dade County Auditorium.

With dance, a great passion in my life was born. I felt a special connection to it, which I enjoyed to the fullest. When I started dancing, it filled me with great spiritual joy. It was almost an awakening. With dance, I started a new life, and through it, I have promoted and honored both life and love.

CHAPTER 11

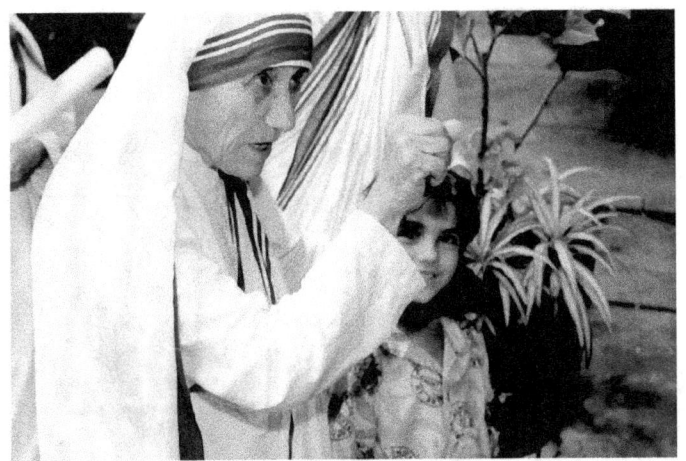
Mother Teresa of Calcutta and Vivian Vanessa. Managua, Nicaragua, 1988.

Mother Teresa of Calcutta, Premonition or Coincidence?

A year before the accident, we were invited to Monsignor Obando y Bravo's home because Mother Teresa of Calcutta was visiting Managua. I attended with my daughter, Vivian Vanessa, and we had the opportunity to meet her. She was a very humble woman, very short in stature, who inspired love and emanated an aura of peace and true serenity.

Shortly before we left, Mother Teresa approached us and, pointing with her index finger, told my daughter, who was only six years old:

"Take good care of your mother because she has a mission in this life."

I listened to her and thought, *Mother Teresa is wrong because I don't have any mission,* and I didn't really believe in her words.

However, a year after that meeting and that phrase, my husband and I, along with 144 other people, were victims of the worst airplane accident in aviation history in Central America. Premonition, coincidence, or clairvoyance ... I don't know, but the truth is that Mother Teresa anticipated my destiny.

That's when my mission began ...

PART II

I intensely lived
the nearness
of death ...
And today,
I intensely live
the blessing
of life!

Vivian Pellas

CHAPTER

1

Vivian dancing "Bamboleo" at Lobo Jack nightclub. Managua, Nicaragua, 1989.

An Inexplicable Fear

On October 19, 1989, Carlos and I flew from Miami to Managua. I was going to participate in a dance show organized by the Diplomatic Ladies and International Missions Association for the benefit of underprivileged children. I hired a professional dancer from Miami, Florida, to design and produce the choreography with the song "Bamboleo" for my performance in Managua.

Dancing gave me another way to express everything I felt and was unable to express with words. I undertook a wonderful journey through this discipline to reach other goals as a woman and as a

> 19 Oct. 1989
> LOBO JACK
> Managua - Nic. —
>
> Presentacion de Bailes Españoles
> por Damas Diplomaticas a Bene-
> ficio obras beneficas.
>
> Vivian Pellas en un pase de
> su calidad Artistica
>
> Dr. Orontes Aviles

"October 19, 1989. Lobo Jack. Managua, Nicaragua.
Spanish dance performance by the Diplomat Ladies for Charity.
Vivian Pellas in a demonstration of her artistic caliber."
Signed, Dr. Orontes Aviles

dancer. It opened my eyes to the wonderful and beautiful life that had been given to me. Dancing was an awakening for me.

It was the first time I would dance in Nicaragua. Nevertheless, a series of premonitions and circumstances began to intrude on my thoughts. Once again, I felt the immense fear of traveling by plane. I was unsure and undecided about this trip. A strange force within me ordered me to stop.

Carlos had to attend a very important meeting of the VISA Board of Directors in Venezuela. After I insisted he travel with me instead of attending his meeting, he agreed, which made me feel a little more secure. I was also looking forward to taking Eduardo, my youngest son, with us. He was only three years old at the time.

AN INEXPLICABLE FEAR

However, I consulted with friends and relatives about this decision, which was inconsistent with my behavior. My mother was of the opinion I should do what I thought was best. My mother-in-law, whom I never called for advice of this kind, suggested the same thing. Then I called my friend Marta Bárcenas, who lived in Costa Rica and had a son Eduardo's age, and her response was identical.

Carlos, frustrated with my hesitation since he had to cancel his trip in advance, didn't want to take Eduardo. Anyway, I still didn't feel reassured. I was eager to dance in Nicaragua, but at the same time, an inner force was preventing me from doing so.

The day before the trip, I decided to go to church. I wanted to be alone to talk to God and ask Him to illuminate me ... and then I had a reassuring moment of contemplation. I looked at the image of Jesus and looked into His eyes. I put my hands together, placed them on my forehead, and confessed. I said, "God, tell me if it's good for me to go on this trip. May Your will be done. Give me courage."

A year earlier, I had told Carlos that, for our children's sake, we should make an effort to travel separately. It was too risky to travel together, considering how often we had been flying. Carlos was not scheduled to come back with me on the return flight. He had already made plans with his friends to go on a fishing tour around Costa Rica, which he had to cancel because the Sandinista Navy did not give him a fishing permit. Therefore, he was forced to reserve a seat on the plane back to Miami with me instead.

The itinerary marked a stopover in Tegucigalpa, Honduras, where my parents were living at that time. That was another of the unforeseen circumstances that occurred before the events that changed the course of our lives. Was it the power of God's supreme force that put my parents on that path so they were close to us at the time of that great tragedy? There were more than a few coincidences like that!

The flight from Miami to Tegucigalpa ran smoothly with little turbulence. We landed and were led to a tiny waiting room at the Toncontín International Airport. My parents were waiting for us. Every time we traveled, we would take advantage of the opportunity to see each other, even from afar, through the glass that divided the rooms. And if we had a chance, we would talk for a few minutes.

That day, I asked the security guard to give me permission to spend a moment with my mother. We went to the ladies' room, and I showed her the beautiful flamenco dress that had been made for me in Miami for my performance in Managua. She enjoyed it when I danced for her despite the limited space in the ladies' room. We hugged each other. She laughed, saying, "The dance is beautiful, Vivian." I went back to the waiting room, and we both left for our respective destinations.

On October 19, I danced at the Lobo Jack nightclub as part of a charity event in Managua. I remember that night as the only time I danced with a strange feeling, which was unfamiliar to me. I always feel alive when I move to the music as I reflect and express many things I feel when I dance. But that evening, I was experiencing different emotions than those my soul wanted to express. I went out to dance with a dark intensity. I didn't understand what was happening to me. That night, I was not myself.

When the choreography was over, I went to the dressing room. My friends joined me there and congratulated me. They said, "Vivian, the way you danced was beautiful," and I said, "I feel as if I hadn't danced at all." I had never felt that dark force inside of me before. I felt like a different person.

It took me two hours to leave the dressing room because I was feeling so strange. Carlos, who was waiting for me inside the nightclub, was very upset and asked me why it took me so long to come out, making him wait. He got even more upset over canceling his trip to Venezuela to come with me to Nicaragua.

In the end, I left downhearted. We didn't celebrate and went straight home.

On the night of October 20, we were invited to have dinner with Carlos's aunts, Adelita and Rosita. Interestingly, during dinner, they insisted, "You two are traveling a lot and always through Honduras. You should know that airport is very dangerous." They repeated their warning when we said goodbye.

I planned to return to Nicaragua in December to celebrate Christmas with family and friends. I didn't say goodbye to anyone, but before leaving home for the airport, on a card addressed to my friend Ena Urcuyo, I wrote:

"Ena, see you in December ... "

When I wrote the last word, I was flooded with immense sadness. I remember I then finished by writing:

"God willing ... "

CHAPTER 2

Airline TAN SAHSA's Boeing 727-200 during its stopover in Costa Rica, before its arrival in Managua on the day of the accident. San José, Costa Rica, October 21, 1989.

"What a Nice Day to Fly!"

On Saturday, October 21, the sky over Managua was bright and very beautiful. We went to the airport, and Carlos said, excited, "What a nice day to fly!"

Those moments are implanted in my memory.

The Boeing 727-200, with thirty-eight passengers on board, took off at six in the morning from the runway of the Juan Santamaría Airport in San José, Costa Rica.

It was approximately 6:35 a.m. when the plane landed in Managua. The stopover wasn't expected to take long, but the number of passengers and the need to refuel the aircraft made the wait longer. Seventy Nicaraguan passengers and thirty of other nationalities boarded the airplane in Managua. Most Nicaraguans were returning to the United States, where they lived, after visiting the families they had left behind years ago, fleeing the upsurge of the war and the hostile conditions the government had made against them.

There were no assigned seats. Therefore, everyone chose where to sit as they pleased. The aircraft did not have first-class seats, but it did have a section with a curtain that separated us from the three front rows where we had wanted to sit. Those seats had already been taken by Dr. Caldera and his wife and by passengers from San José, one of them Curt Schaeffer, to whom the flight attendant had given the window seat on the right side of the third row.

Carlos and I sat in the front-row seats behind the division. He sat by the aisle, and I took the window seat, leaving the middle seat empty. The last passengers to enter the plane were Camilo René Castellón Estrada and his wife, Irene García Argüello de Castellón, parents of the poet Blanquita Castellón. I asked Carlos to move to the middle seat so that Don Castellón could take the aisle seat. That way, he could be closer to his wife, who was in the first seat across the aisle.

Carlos didn't like my suggestion because he preferred the aisle seat. He asked me to move to the middle so Mr. Castellón could take the window seat. So, we did, and in the end, the Castellóns sat separately.

The couple had been living in the United States since the Nicaraguan government confiscated their property. They returned that year, 1989, to register for and participate in the 1990 elections. They were excited about the euphoria caused by the opposition candidacy of Violeta Barrios de Chamorro. This would give them the possibility of returning to their longed-for homeland. That was the desire of many exiled Nicaraguans, who finally came back with the election victory of the National Opposition Union (UNO) party, which promised a change for the country.

Hope was reborn for the Nicaraguan people while life was preparing a new setback for us.

CHAPTER

Remains of TAN SAHSA's Boeing 727-200 after the accident at Cerro de Hula. Tegucigalpa, Honduras, October 1989.

Flight 414: An Encounter with Death

Honduran airline TAN SAHSA Flight 414 took off that sunny morning with a delay of only a few minutes since it took longer for some passengers to board the plane. The flight attendants gave their standard instructions, which included security measures. Only 134 miles (215 km) separated us from Tegucigalpa, which meant we would land at Toncontín in 25 or 30 minutes at around 8:00 a.m.

Fifteen minutes after takeoff and reaching eighteen thousand feet (5486 m), as we left the western volcanic chain behind and entered the

Remains of the Boeing 727-200, after the accident at Cerro de Hula. Tegucigalpa, Honduras, October 1989.

mountainous area of Honduras, the weather suddenly started to change. Although it was cloudy, the aircraft advanced without turbulence. The sky was a huge gray mass. I couldn't see anything, and that made me feel afraid. After a few minutes, the weather returned to normal again. The flight attendant took the microphone to announce we were near the Toncontín International Airport.

At that instant, we felt the airplane descend sharply and disappear into a dark cloud. At that moment, I thought, *We are going to die*, as sadness invaded my entire being. I immediately closed my eyes and felt what I had always feared was coming true. I thought there was no way out and realized my premonition had just materialized.

Salió disparado en el sillón

EMPRESARIO ESPAÑOL RELATA EL ACCIDENTE

MANAGUA, Oct. 21 (AFP).- El empresario español Carlos Pellas, sobreviviente del accidente aéreo ocurrido hoy al sur de Tegucigalpa, relató que, "de pronto el avión se partió en dos, salí disparado atado al sillón y vi cómo el aparato estalló en llamas segundos después".

Aún aturdido por la tragedia y con la voz entrecortada, Pellas, —empresario con fuertes inversiones en Nicaragua y el resto de Centroamérica— narró a la emisora local La Voz de Nicaragua cómo salió "catapultado" del Boeing 727 y chocó contra el follaje.

Sin perder el conocimiento, miró desde tierra estrellarse al avión, dentro del cual estaba inconsciente su esposa Miriam. Rápidamente se dirigió al aparato, desprendió a su mujer, la cargó y mientras se alejaba con ella el avión explotó.

"Todo fue en cuestión de segundos. Es algo horrible", expresó el empresario español, que vela por los intereses económicos de su familia, uno de las más poderosas de Centroamérica.

Pellas no supo precisar por qué el piloto decidió hacer un aterrizaje de emergencia en una plaza de fútbol del municipio de San Buenaventura, en las faldas del cerro Hula, unos 40 Km. al sur de Tegucigalpa.

Según Pellas, el piloto no dio ninguna explicación a los pasajeros sobre lo que estaba ocurriendo.

"Únicamente escuché un ruido y el avión se partió en dos", detalló.

Mientras tanto, las oficinas de Migración y los alrededores de la embajada hondureña en esta capital vivieron esta mañana escenas desgarradoras, cuando decenas de familiares de las víctimas se agruparon en busca de información.

Un total de 65 nicaragüenses abordaron esta mañana el fatídico vuelo de SAHSA que hizo escala en Managua, procedente de Costa Rica, y se estima que la mayoría de ellos figurarían entre los más de 120 muertos.

Histérica y casi sin poder atinar palabras, la madre de una joven nicaragüense recordó cómo su hija, que estaba en lista de espera la llamó por teléfono y le dijo: "Mamá, yo me monto en ese avión aunque sea en la cola".

Y efectivamente logró cupo dentro del vuelo fatal.

La lista de pasajeros del avión accidentado

TEGUCIGALPA / AP

Pasajeros de cuando menos 16 nacionalidades figuraron en el avión hondureño que se accidentó el sábado al sur de esta capital, ocasionando la muerte de por lo menos 132 personas.

Ello se desprende de las listas de pasajeros que abordaron el avión Boeing 727-200 de la empresa Tan-Sahsa en San José, Costa Rica y Nicaragua, que terminó estrellándose en una montaña al sur de Tegucigalpa.

Las listas, entregadas por Alfonso Valladares, gerente de reservaciones de la aerolínea en Honduras, no están completas, debido a que la suma de pasajeros llega a 125 y figuran entre éstos algunos mencionados por las autoridades como sobrevivientes.

La lista de sobrevivientes tampoco ha sido definitiva, ya que la empresa hondureña dijo que ha cerrado sus actividades de la jornada.

La compañía dijo inicialmente que el avión transportaba 164 personas, luego indicó que eran menos y que se había comprobado la muerte de 131 de ellas.

En las listas, figuran 59 nicaragüenses, 34 hondureños, 11 de Estados Unidos, cuatro de Francia, cuatro de España, dos de Suecia y uno de Perú, Bélgica, la Unión Soviética, Bolivia, Checoslovaquia, Chile, Argentina, Finlandia y Gran Bretaña.

Las listas: pasajeros embarcados en San José, Costa Rica. Estadounidenses: 1. Robert Heyr, 2. Eugennee van Dicke, 3. Curtis Shaffer, 4. Marie Apodaca, 5. Edward Apodaca. Nicaragüenses: Franklin Davis. Peruanos: 1. Hermes Coloma. Costarricenses: 1. Mario Rodríguez. Hondureños: 1. Diana Pozzen, 2. Vilma Laínez, 3. Fanny Sánchez, 4. María Ulloa, 5. Omar Zavala, 6. Tomasa Valle, 7. Dagoberto Guillén, 8. Roberto Zúñiga, 9. Ricardo Heerez, 10. María Oquelí, 11. José Pascuel, 12. Rolando Barahona, 13. Gardel Cáceres, 14. Edmundo Ayala, 15. Raquel Mateo, 16. Francisca Canales, 17. Augusto Cárcamo, 18. Martha Banegas, 19. César Montes, 20. Eventir López, 21. Luis Portillo, 22. Hernán Madrid.

Pasajeros embarcados en Nicaragua. Nicaragüenses: 1. Harry Vega, 2. Carlos Vega, 3. Jazmín Reyes, 4. Margarita Aben, 5. María Torres, 6. Tatiana Torres, 7. Patricia Torres, 8. Francisco Espinoza, 9. Vigarini González, 10. Purificación Bizzo, 11. Rina Flores, 12. José López, 13. Ana Silva, 14. Martha Ramírez, 15. Sr. Villalobos (sin identificar plenamente aún).

The Miami Herald

MONDAY, OCTOBER 23, 1983

131 killed in Honduran jet crash

Airliner breaks apart, hits mountain; 15 survive

The grating sound of the tremendous impact horrified us as we crashed in the blink of an eye. We saw a big fireball coming toward us. Carlos remembers the expression of panic on my face. In deep despair, he silently prayed, *My God, forgive me for all my sins and protect my children ...*

I was unconscious from then on. Carlos never lost consciousness and had a clear mind the whole time. He remembers the screams, the crying, the anguish, the scenes of panic among the passengers ...

The plane took giant leaps like a huge fly as it touched the ground, breaking into pieces and razing everything in its path. And then, the first explosion occurred.

Everything started to darken. Billowing clouds of black smoke made it hard to breathe. Carlos was catapulted out of the aircraft. He got up in confusion, but in a split second, he remembered me and returned to the burning plane with his hands, arms, face, and feet seared.

He entered through a chasm in the middle of a fireball as the flames devoured the entire fuselage, which had now become a mass of metal. I was unconscious and restrained by the belt that was asphyxiating me against the seat, which had detached from the floor and fallen onto the fuselage of the plane. Carlos was yelling, "Viviaaaaaaaan!"

Amidst the mutilated and totally charred bodies and almost unconscious passengers, Carlos continued to look for me, crossing through the fire

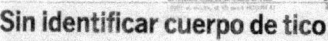

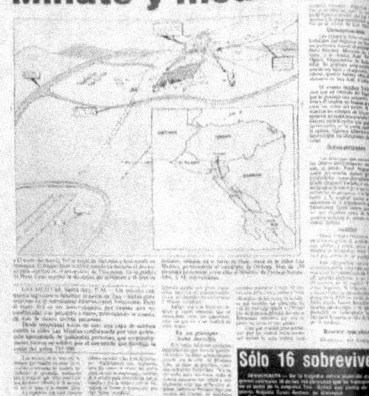

Scenes of the accident at Cerro de Hula. Tegucigalpa, Honduras, October 1989.

that blocked his path. There, he saw a woman trapped by the hot iron. She was still moaning.

Meanwhile, I was more dead than alive. All of a sudden, I heard Carlos's voice screaming my name in the distance, and that brought me out of my stupor for a few moments. Finally, he recognized me for the blue and white shirt I was wearing that day since my face was already completely disfigured. He talked to me, screamed at me, as he tried to unbuckle my seatbelt, but his hands were so burned he couldn't do it.

Unable to unfasten my seatbelt, he continued to scream in anguish. Suddenly, he realized his left hand was completely burnt. At that very instant, I was falling into an abyss. I made several attempts to come to life again, and in that last effort, I heard Carlos

LA PRENSA

60 PÁGINAS
VALE 40 CTVS
TIRAJE DE HOY
41,891
EJEMPLARES

EL DIARIO INDEPENDIENTE DE MAYOR CIRCULACIÓN EN HONDURAS
MIEMBRO DE LA SOCIEDAD INTERAMERICANA DE PRENSA (SIP)

AÑO XXV — SAN PEDRO SULA, MARTES 24 DE OCTUBRE DE 1989 — N 12873

2 mil refugiados regresan hoy a El Salvador
Inf. Pag. 9

Error humano habría causado accidente

* 131 muertos y 15 sobrevivientes, cifras oficiales.
* Ministro de Defensa identifica a su hija.

Mientras los barriles se recuperan y los parientes han identificado decenas de cadáveres, las labores de rescate en Las Mesitas quedó deteñida, por lo que Aeronáutica Civil pidió a Salud que inicie la desinfestación de la zona. En las gráficas, arriba, maquinaria pesada trabaja en área del desastre. Abajo, una joven rompe el momento de despedida al momento de sepultar a la hondureña Diane Pozzo Tamez. (Fotos Osman Gaona, Inf. Pags. 4, 5, 12, 13, 56 y 57)

En Celina:
Inicia tiraje de votos
Inf. Pág. 2

Regresa el Atlantis
Inf. Pág. 35

Los secuestran y dejan desnudos y atados en cañales
Inf. Págs. 10 y 11

Serios daños causa mal tiempo en Zona Atlántica
Inf. Pág. 3

8A MONDAY, OCTOBER 23, 1989
THE MIAMI HERALD

AROUND THE AMERICAS

Demand outstrips seats for flights to Honduras

Miami crowded with people trying to get to crash site

By CHRISTOPHER MARQUIS
Herald Staff Writer

Grieving relatives and held-over travelers converged at Miami International Airport Sunday, competing for scarce seats to Honduras a day after 131 people died there in a mountainside crash.

Officials with Honduras' TAN-SAHSA airline frantically added through demands from families, aviation authorities and scores of travelers stranded since Saturday's early morning wreck.

Dozens at ticket holders for TAN-SAHSA flights to the capital, Tegucigalpa, were turned away at the counter Sunday afternoon.

One of them was Carmen Matos.

A small curly-haired woman with an 11-year-old son in tow, Matos stared at the ticket agent with red-ringed eyes.

"I am living a nightmare," she muttered.

The tragic phone call came Saturday afternoon. Her big sister, Rayzel, 58 — "Isn't it strange, it's always the fave one, the favorite daughter" — was dead.

Since then there was no sleep, "not a wink," as Matos borrowed a car in Goshen, Ind., where she was taking a course in English. Fort Wayne, Ind., to Nashville, Tenn., to

Miami. All was rush. Her eyes like had stopped.

"I haven't changed any clothes since yesterday."

She looked at her son, dressed in a mauve U.S. Navy flight jacket, sitting still with preteenaged thoughts.

"He (her dad when I was four months pregnant," she said, sombrered. "I guess it feels the same every time."

Matos said she would return to Tegucigalpa to help stow her sister's three children.

But not right away. She was handed back her ticket — and a voucher for a night at the Airport Ramada Inn.

The airline declined to say how many relatives of crash victims in Miami had accepted their offer of a free flight to Honduras.

Meanwhile, U.S. insurance adjusters and Federal Aviation Administration officials sought to investigate the cause of the crash, which left spare cockpit seats.

One aviation source, George Delgado, said the accident appeared to be caused by human error, either in the cockpit or in air traffic control.

The "black box" flight recorder had been recovered, Delgado said, and was being handed over to the National Transportation Safety Board in Miami.

Still, crash witnesses told reporters that the plane was on fire before it slammed into a 6,000 foot mountain near Las Tablitas. The chief of

FEATURED:

(list of Americans aboard flight, names partially legible)

Washington D.C.
Gregory Pagin, U.S. Marine stationed in Washington, and the U.S. Embassy in Tegucigalpa, son Duncan who survived the crash. "The Embassy said it assistance was known. The reader went a military police identification of families.

SURVIVORS:
Eugene Van Dyke, U.S. Agency for International Development employee in Tegucigalpa, wife of the crash. Michael O'Shea, Costa Rica, Ivana Nissen.

"Those planes are old.
And they really take a beating landing in Tegucigalpa."

TAN-SAHSA AIRLINE OFFICIAL

civil aeronautics in Nicaragua, Max Alejandro Agustín, cited contributory reports that part of the fuselage was torn off during the flight.

A TAN-SAHSA official in Miami, who spoke on the condition he not be named, said rocky terrain likely caused the plane to fall apart.

"Those planes are old," he said. "And they really take a beating landing in Tegucigalpa."

The crash occurred at Cerro Hules, about 25 miles south of Tegucigalpa. The Boeing 727-200 was 21 years old, said the manufacturer.

Among frequent travelers, Hondurans' main airport is known for bumpy approaches and abrupt landings. Wind shears and fog, a common over the mountainous terrain, and the airport's runways are unusually short.

"I swore on my last flight I'd never fly into that airport again," the airline official said.

GRIM TASK: Two women builds the odor at Tegucigalpa's morgue where they tried to identify the bodies of relatives Sunday.

insistently say, "Viviaaaannn ... " I felt myself coming back to life, inch by inch, like a tree that recovers its strength from the roots up. I managed to open my eyes and could see, in the middle of the fire, the figure of Carlos, in flames, grabbing his head. He shouted at me again and threw himself on top of me until he managed to unfasten my seatbelt. As he lifted me up strongly, he said: "Vivian, take a leap and follow me!"

Carlos evacuated the plane. In my daze, amidst the flames, dense smoke, and extreme heat caused by the numerous explosions, I saw a window of transparent and crystalline light at my feet. It was something undefinable. I have only seen that light that illuminated my feet on the print of the Lord of Divine Mercy. I felt like I was descending through a black tunnel as my eyes closed.

All of a sudden, I came back to myself and bounced out of what was left of the aircraft as if someone or something was pushing me. I explored my body to see if I still had hands and legs. I could see that my feet were shattered. My fingernails and my skin, unbelievably, had totally melted. They hung to the ground! Suddenly, I glimpsed a rainbow before me. I don't know where it came from; it could have been my imagination, but I remembered my children, and then ... I started running.

Sometime later, Carlos remembered the first thought that came to his mind after the impact: *We had to get out of that hell—both or one of us!* At least one of us had to be saved for our children, who were three, seven, and ten years old at that time. We couldn't leave them alone.

I looked back, and at that very moment, the plane exploded. The force of the shock wave lifted me into the air. I flew over Carlos, down the hill, and fell on a rock. My body was somehow broken. I tried to get up several times, but I couldn't. Then I saw a figure moving. I assumed it was Carlos, but perhaps it was a mirage.

Instinctively, I pushed something over my shoulder with my hand. Only then could I stand up. I wanted to get up and run, but I collapsed at every attempt. Later, I learned my collarbone was fractured when I fell, and what I was pushing was my bone so I could get up.

A piece of hot iron was buried in my right foot, melting my skin to the bone. Carlos told me that then, with much effort and desperation, we had to get away from the airplane by walking through a cornfield. We rolled over rocks with shattered feet and through a horrible cold that pierced right to our bones since they no longer had any skin. This was something beyond terrible ... totally indescribable!

I fell repeatedly as we went down the mountain. I was breathless, barefoot, skinless, and frozen. I tried to get up, but I lacked strength. Carlos picked me up over and over again. I remember I could see three or four figures with rags wound around their heads. They were some old women shrouded by the fog and the semi-darkness of that nameless dawn.

They were, no doubt, horrified by the Dantesque images unfolding before their eyes ... and we were the protagonists!

I could see that the airplane was totally engulfed in flames, and there we were, in the middle of the countryside, with a frost that touched our very souls despite the proximity of the fire. It felt as if we had been immersed in the underworld. It was a surreal moment in our lives. I have no other way to describe it.

The panorama was devastating. Fire, smoke, twisted iron, and chunks of the plane were scattered all over the area. We saw arms, hands, legs, incinerated bodies ... some even hanging from the branches of the trees. Pleading, death found them in their last prayer, with their faces transfigured by horror and their stony gazes transfixed on the sky.

The destruction impacted the vegetation for a radius equivalent to five city blocks. What was left of the charred trees and plants was impregnated with the stench of jet fuel and burnt flesh ...

And in the background, the whisper of the wind carried the laments of the few survivors.

CHAPTER

4

Vivian's father and Carlos Vásquez, owner of the truck, and his family. Tegucigalpa, Honduras, 1989.

An Angel on the Mountain

We did not see the accident coming. For some inexplicable reason, the pilots did not follow the instructions, and it was too late when they tried to lift the plane from its descent: the aircraft crashed into Cerro de Hula, a hill near the village of Las Mesitas, only 19 miles (30.5 km) from Toncontín International Airport.

The black box revealed that the plane was flying extremely low despite the navigation system's warnings to regain altitude. It is beyond comprehension why the pilots ignored the controls' warnings.

It was clear that human error caused the accident, and there we were, in the middle of hell, fighting to escape it.

On the way down the mountain, Carlos found an old single cab truck abandoned by the side of the road. He tried to scream, but he could only get out a mumble because of all the smoke he had inhaled. He was calling for help. Almost a mile away, on the other side of the road, we saw a small, humble dwelling.

Suddenly, a farmer appeared, horrified by the scraping sound of the impact. Carlos approached him and asked whose truck it was. The man said it was his. Carlos immediately asked him to take us to a hospital, and the man, in shock, told him it was in bad condition and had no gasoline. Carlos never lost his composure and insisted, "Look, I'll pay for it, but please take us to the hospital."

The farmer was pale and totally out of control. He regained his composure and went to get the key to drive us. Then he told Carlos he thought it was the end of the world, and that's why he ran towards the crash site when he heard the explosion.

The local farmers used that flight as their clock every day. The airplane's passage set the time for their children to leave for school. But that day, the airplane did not fly over them ... and the long-awaited sound transformed into one of the most overwhelming scenes, terrorizing them for years to come.

Only a few small houses were dotting the hill. At that moment, other survivors were coming down the

Truck in which Vivian, Carlos, and other injured passengers were transported from Cerro de Hula to Escuela Hospital. Tegucigalpa, Honduras, 1989.

mountainside. Their condition was awful. Confused, we wondered if that was how we looked. My awareness was altered, and a blanket of unreality distorted my perception of everything around me.

Years later, Curt Schaeffer, Ramón Sánchez Borba, may he rest in peace, and Evenor López told us about their own odyssey. Curt had been ejected from the plane, thrown through the air with his seat and his seatbelt still fastened. He landed alone in the middle of a field since he had fallen from the other side of the plane. He did not see any survivors or bodies.

The state of shock stunned him for a few minutes, leaving him unable to react. He then saw a group of farmers in a cornfield. He called for help, but no one came to his aid. He and Carlos could not explain this behavior since, in these cases, the nature of human beings is to help.

The faces of the farmers could not mask their horror, as if they were witnessing a terrifying scene. They were all petrified. Little by little, Curt stood up after managing to unbuckle his seatbelt. With his body lacerated, he took a few steps toward the farmers and signaled for help, but no one paid any attention to him.

He decided to walk and had to make his way through thick bushes. He fell in the mud and moved forward with great difficulty. He pushed on to a small adobe house about 700 feet (213 m) downhill. He walked in and saw an old woman emerging from the smoke of the wood stove. He asked for help, and she offered him water. He left the house to continue walking down the mountainside.

Evenor López took the flight in San José after participating, along with his friend Hernán Madrid, in a seminar promoted by the Instituto Centroamericano de Administración de Empresas (INCAE). He was sitting in the fourth row and had been sleeping until the voice of the flight attendant woke him up, asking him to fasten his seatbelt.

Ramón Sánchez Borba was returning from Nicaragua after providing legal advice to Teddy Norman, who was traveling with him. He traveled all the time, given the demands of his legal practice. Mr. Sánchez Borba was sitting in the front row.

Near the end of the flight, he told his neighbor it was always cloudy near Tegucigalpa. At that very moment, the man shouted, "This plane is falling!" and, all of a sudden, they felt the impact. He never saw his partner again. The thick smoke pushed him back, and he walked to the back of the airplane, where he found an opening.

He jumped out of the plane, and the explosion forced him to move away. He felt the stinging pain of the burns. He couldn't breathe because his lungs were full of smoke. He walked a little, but the pain prevented him from continuing until some men helped him get to a school.

Farther ahead was the dilapidated truck that would become his hope for life.

CHAPTER 5

Escuela Hospital. Tegucigalpa, Honduras, 1989.

Skinless

In moments of the greatest anguish, you never imagine where your salvation will come from.

There we were ... fighting for our lives! Carlos and I got in the truck's cabin. Later, we saw other survivors: Curt Schaeffer, Ramón Sánchez Borba, Erika, the flight attendant, a couple of Australians, the pilot, and the co-pilot. All of them got into the back of the truck.

We started the trip on a dirt road in very bad condition. Sometimes, it looked like mountainous terrain. At times, the trail became generous and had mercy on our torn bodies. Carlos would ask the driver to speed up because he knew we were in very serious condition and that we might die soon.

At the same time, the passengers in the back would shout, pleading for the driver to slow down because the cold wind caused them more pain as it penetrated their skinless bodies since the truck had no canopy. This was the moment when Carlos thought I would not survive.

The pain made me turn around, and by chance, I caught my image reflected in the rearview mirror. I could see a hole in my face that made my back teeth visible. I could only moan. I couldn't speak. My jaw was broken.

Carlos mumbled, "Vivian, we will need eight to nine months in the hospital." To console us, and with great effort, I was able to whisper, "Don't worry, this will take two or three days." At that moment, I thought, *There is nothing more distressing than feeling that you are going to die.*

Carlos's hands were shattered. He couldn't touch anything. His head was charred. Without considering the survivors in the back of the truck, Carlos again asked the driver to speed up. However, it was impossible to go any faster. Once again, the screams of pain made our souls tremble. The path became muddy, and the jerking movements of the truck through the potholes were enough to cause the wailing. We were all suffering too much. It was indescribable.

As we went down the mountain a little farther ahead, we saw a family of farmers walking on the

Cabin of the truck in which Carlos and Vivian were transported from the crash site to Escuela Hospital. Tegucigalpa, Honduras, 1989.

hillside. Their faces clearly displayed shock after seeing ours. After an hour of torture, we finally reached the road.

We knew we were close to the city from the vehicle traffic. We heard the desperate wailing of ambulance, fire truck, and police car sirens. Some of them passed in front of us without noticing the load of dying wounded that our "improvised ambulance" was carrying. We passed by the airport. *What irony*, I thought. *My parents must be waiting for us in one of its rooms.* To make matters worse, the capital was more congested than usual.

The traffic was suffocating. That day was Honduran Armed Forces Day. The driver was disoriented and didn't know the route he was supposed to take. He would stop to ask directions. Carlos told him to stop a taxi and ask the driver to take us to Escuela Hospital because that was what came to his mind at that moment.

Other vehicles would pass by near us, and a grimace of horror transformed the faces of their curious occupants as they saw the apocalyptic picture of the injured in the dilapidated truck. They would immediately look away, grab their heads in fear, slow down for a few seconds, and continue on their way.

At last, we reached Escuela Hospital. At the gate to the emergency entrance, an avalanche of street vendors blocked the way, and the doctors, already aware of the news, were waiting for the wounded from the plane crash. The only stretcher was for me because I was the one in the worst condition. Little by little, we learned more about the events that had transpired as we suffered the ravages of having survived the plane crash.

Radio stations and television programs interrupted their broadcasts to report the event. My parents and the relatives who were waiting at the airport knew nothing about it. When they noticed the flight was delayed and without any information from the airline staff, they began to worry. Mother said to my father, "Pepe, let's go, it looks like the plane didn't stop in Honduras, and they continued straight to Miami."

They arrived at their home, and within minutes, a phone call informed them of the disaster.

Carlos Vásquez, the driver and owner of the rickety truck, told my mother how he had taken us to the hospital. My husband, who had remained completely lucid at all times, had given him their home phone number and asked him to call her.

"Are you Doña Lydia Fernández?" Carlos Vásquez asked. "Yes, that's me. Who is this?"

"Ma'am, your children were in the airplane that crashed into Cerro de Hula, and they are in Escuela Hospital."

"This can't be true. You're playing a joke on me!" my mother shouted.

"No, ma'am, your children were in a plane accident. The plane crashed into a mountain, and they are in the hospital!"

That was just the first dose of pain for my mom on that nameless day. The time ahead would test her unyielding strength ... as well as ours.

CHAPTER 6

Vivian and her mother. Managua, Nicaragua, 1974.

"My Child, What Happened to You?!"

You never know when misfortune will knock at your door. The devastating news shattered my mother's composure.

After the call from Carlos Vásquez, the man who helped us, my mother was inconsolable. She threw the phone away and, screaming, ran to find my father. Escuela Hospital was just a few minutes away from their home.

When they arrived at the emergency room, my mom said, "Pepe, you go to Carlos, and I'll go to see

Vivian." Dad was shocked to see how Carlos's skin, and even his fingernails, were hanging from his body. His eyes were closed because his face was completely swollen. My mother was anxiously looking for me and finally found me at the other end of the room. She approached me when I was expelling black vomit from the smoke I had inhaled.

My entire body was one huge, painful sore. The swelling was so severe that the wedding ring on my right hand became an unbearable source of torture. No matter how much lubricant they rubbed on my finger, they couldn't get it off. Dr. Edmundo del Carmen brought a special pincer for cutting bones. The pain caused by the pressure they had to exert made me scream, and I almost fainted.

All the bones in my face were fractured. I had more than sixty fractures and multiple injuries all over my face. Mom wanted to come close to me, but they wouldn't let her. Countless doctors and nurses surrounded the stretcher. With the strength of a mother's despair, she pushed them all away and shouted, "That's my daughter!" They made way for her, and once she was by my side, she said, "My child, what happened to you?!" At that moment, I lost consciousness ... I knew she was with me.

According to all the media reports, other wounded were treated at the same hospital. American Deborah Lea Browning and Ramón Sánchez Borba, a Paraguayan-born national of Honduras, were later transferred to Viera Hospital. American Curt

"MY CHILD, WHAT HAPPENED TO YOU?!"

Schaeffer was transferred to La Policlínica Hospital and then to the United States.

The hospital corridor was packed with doctors, nurses, and curious bystanders. Desperate families waited impatiently for the arrival of other survivors. We were put in separate rooms, and with every scream, every cry, or every call to a patient's family over the speakers, Carlos, terrified, would ask if I was alright. He heard the typical calm female voice in hospitals calling a person's relatives. A woman died on a stretcher next to Carlos. He thought it might have been me. He asked the nurses, and they denied it. Carlos told Dr. Del Carmen, who was treating him, that he didn't believe anyone. He stood up with all the tubes in his arms, anguished and in disbelief since he thought no one was telling him the truth. He was able to confirm that the lady who died was the flight attendant, Erika Williams. She did not suffer any major external burns but did suffer internal ones, which caused her death.

According to one of Erika Williams's colleagues, she did not fully trust Captain Argueta. She even told her if something bad ever happened one day, it would be because of that pilot.

Furthermore, the day before the accident, Erika told her colleague she had a premonition that something "bad" was going to happen. Erika received reassurances, but she continued to insist on the fact that she had a bad feeling ...

Minutes after Erika's death, an unidentified boy with burns on 90% of his body died as well. Many investigations about the boy and his identity were carried out, but all of them were unsuccessful.

The worst predicament Carlos went through while almost dying was the constant badgering he was subjected to in order to find out his nationality. All those who approached him asked the same thing. Many desperate relatives, not receiving information about whether there were other survivors, decided to take matters into their hands and go to Cerro de Hula to search for their loved ones on their own. With an experienced driver who knew the terrain, they could get there in an hour, more or less.

Once they arrived at the site, they found out that all the survivors had been transferred to different assistance centers in Tegucigalpa. A few were assisted by other farmers in the area and then had to wait at a school near the disaster site. Rescue services did not arrive immediately, given the rugged terrain and difficult access and because the corresponding authorities had not officially confirmed the news.

A public bus that went through the different surrounding areas was passing by the hill at that time and transported some of the injured. On the way, they came across several ambulances, and the passengers were transferred.

The survivors that were part of the crew were captain and pilot Raul Argueta, co-pilot Reiniero Canales, and flight attendants Nivia Umanzor and

Guiomar Nuñez. Other survivors were the Honduran Hernán Madrid, Americans Jean Van Dike and Curt Schaeffer, Dr. Ramón Sánchez Borba, and the Australian couple Ronald and Helen Deveraux, among others. The manager of the TAN SAHSA terminal in Managua did not have the same luck. He was in the cockpit because there were no empty seats on the flight. He was the last person to board, and with the impact, his body was thrown about 700 feet (213 m) away from the spot where the plane crashed, dying instantly.

Putting this together with other circumstances recounted by other passengers before the trip, I can safely say that premonitions surrounded Flight 414. These conjectures have no logical explanation but are consistent and miraculous when they are assembled and connected in one story.

Curt Schaeffer collects testimonies of families who lost loved ones and the stories of some of the survivors in his book *Escape With One's Life*, published in 2005. These stories made me remember the feeling I had before I took the TAN SAHSA flight. We had been traveling a lot, and I was afraid we might have an accident. I told Carlos we needed to start flying separately, and we did so on the last trips we made back then. In the case of the day of the accident, Carlos was traveling with me because the permit he needed to fish in Costa Rica was denied. Life is strange! By the grace of God and because of him, I was able to write this book.

The radio was still broadcasting news of the incident. Neither TAN SAHSA nor the airport officials could hide what was already so obvious any longer. Some of the porters at the airport knew about the event, and the news spread even faster.

Dr. Edmundo del Carmen, a Nicaraguan surgeon and pulmonologist and also a childhood friend of Carlos and my brother Alejandro, was working as a doctor at Escuela Hospital. When he finished his specialia specialization studies in Mexico, he decided to settle down in Tegucigalpa, and there he married Myrna Hasbum to start a family.

The morning of the accident, he received a message from the private medical center he worked for. They asked him to come urgently to treat some injured people without knowing they had been through the air tragedy. His sister, Inés de Zablah, sent him a message at 8:30 a.m. to let him know about the accident as well.

A sister of his father-in-law, who was living in Lima, had been in Honduras for a two-week vacation and took the opportunity to visit some relatives in Nicaragua. She was returning on that plane and died in the crash. His father-in-law contacted the doctor, asking for his support.

Almost at the same time, he received six messages on his beeper from my father, who asked him to call him back. Edmundo was like a son to my parents. He was a few blocks from Escuela Hospital when he heard the news on the radio saying the first survivors of

"MY CHILD, WHAT HAPPENED TO YOU?!"

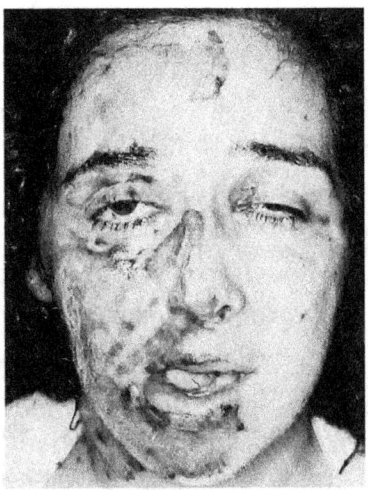

Vivian after several surgical interventions a few months after the accident. Miami, Florida, 1989.

the accident had been taken to that hospital and "that they were citizens of Spanish origin, whose names were Carlos Peláez Chamorro and Vivian de Peláez." He immediately associated those last names with my father's calls. He made a quick left turn and drove straight to the hospital. He left the car half a block away. When he arrived, he found a crowd blocking the entrance to the center, trying to get information about their relatives.

He rushed to the emergency room, where he saw my mother, her face filled with anguish: "*Mundo*, the kids are over there ... Help us!"

He recognized us as soon as he saw us. His professionalism prevailed in coping with the pain of seeing us in such a condition. He checked Carlos and me, evaluating the state of the burns. He then told Carlos we needed to be taken to the operating room for surgical cleaning. Carlos, who was very concerned, said, "Please see Vivian first."

The medical team included Dr. Del Carmen, plastic surgeon César Enríquez, and anesthesiologist Xenia Pineda, who arrived as volunteers on call at the hospital, although they were not on duty. Dr. Pineda had studied her specialty with Dr. Del Carmen, and they had a good longstanding working relationship and friendship. Amidst the chaos and with only two of the hospital's fourteen operating rooms functioning, Dr. Del Carmen decided to start providing care to us because he knew it was a long process.

Moreover, if more wounded came in, everything would become more complicated. After reviewing x-rays, vital signs, and blood pressure, making sure there was no other critical condition that could put our lives at risk beyond the burns, we were taken to the operating room to start the surgical cleaning.

In addition to the trauma caused by my wedding ring, the watch I was wearing burned my arm, although, curiously, it was still working. The silver bracelet near my right hand had melted with the fire and was injuring me as it pressed against my wrist. My mom received everything that was left of these objects.

Luckily, that day, I was wearing jeans, and their fabric protected my legs. If I had worn nylon stockings, I would have been burned as much as the flight attendants.

Once in the operating room, they started cleaning me up. I listened to the doctors discuss whether or not they could use anesthesia. They wanted to know if I had eaten breakfast during the flight. I couldn't talk to them. Finally, they decided to operate on me, but the vomiting continued very strongly. I was expelling a strange black substance through my mouth and nose from the large amount of smoke I had inhaled.

A serious mishap occurred as soon as anesthesia was administered. Since I had indeed eaten breakfast, the vomiting complicated the situation. The anesthesiologist immediately turned my head and aspirated me to prevent the gastric contents from going into my lungs. It would have been catastrophic. She acted with incredible reflexes to save my life with that maneuver.

Once I was anesthetized, the first thing Dr. Enríquez did was to sew up the external wounds on my face and neck. As I would say later, it was kind of a "war repair." With the help of a large group of doctors, Dr. Enríquez instructed each of them to take one part of my body and, simultaneously, to rub and wash the entire burned area until the skin was pink and raw, and that way, all the necrotic areas were removed.

They cleaned the wounds deeply with a brush because any burned skin remaining in the pores can cause infection. After working on my face, they continued with my torso and finished with my legs. This was an emergency debridement process that lasted over two hours.

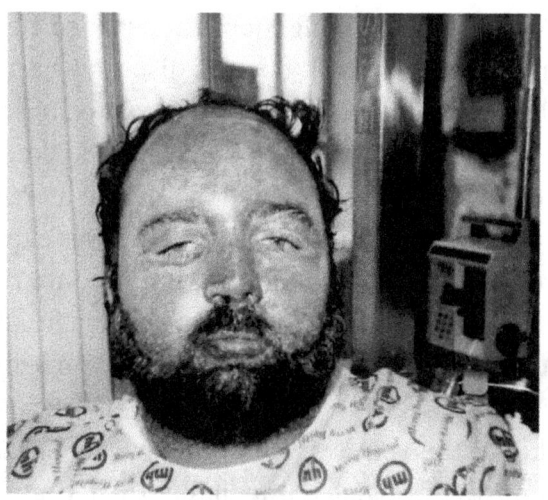

Carlos Pellas, weeks after the accident at Mercy Hospital. Miami, Florida, 1989.

As soon as they were done, Dr. Del Carmen told Carlos they had finished the cleaning and that I was "fine." Carlos mumbled: "Thank God!"

Carlos had very delicate burns on his face, neck, feet, hands, and arms. His face was completely swollen, almost like a full moon. Before he was put to sleep, he asked to speak to Dr. Del Carmen and said, "If I die, my last wish is that my in-laws become the legal guardians of my children and that they take care of them." He asked the doctor to write down the insurance number, "in case it's necessary." He made the sign of the cross and said, "Proceed."

When she was about to start intubating him, the anesthesiologist realized it was not going to be possible to carry out the procedure because Carlos's neck and nose were too swollen. Dr. Del Carmen muttered to Dr. Pineda, "My friend did not die in the accident, and I don't want him to die from edema caused by intubation. Let's not give him general anesthesia. Let's sedate him and go with a mask and intravenous medication."

The sedation was supposed to work for an hour, and then oxygen would have to be added to keep him half awake. After two attempts, Dr. Pineda was shocked to find that sedation lasted only fifteen minutes, which was not enough time to perform Carlos's debridement. He woke up eight times during the entire process. Dr. Del Carmen later explained that Carlos had a fast metabolism, and therefore, he eliminated the medication in a short period of time.

They practiced surgical cleaning on each part of his body in stages and for the duration of each sedation until the cleaning was completed a couple of hours later. After that, he was taken to the recovery room. However, the doctors felt it was necessary to amputate the left hand. They would wait for the reaction to the cleaning to make a final decision. However, amputation was almost a fact.

Dr. Del Carmen said as soon as Carlos opened his eyes, he asked about me. I was in the same room, but he didn't know where I was. Then, they placed me by his side. He looked back at me and remembers saying, "Hi, honey." He blew a kiss and went back to sleep. It is incredible how Carlos always had a clear mind.

I was in very bad condition. They had no idea of the internal damage to my face. My case was much more serious than Carlos's. My face was totally disfigured.

The next step was to move us to a special room since there was a risk of infection that every burn patient could suffer if not isolated, along with the need to replenish fluids and electrolytes lost during the burn. We were given intravenous fluids, plasma infusion, antibiotics, a tetanus vaccine, and strong painkillers. All of this was under strict observation.

Fortunately, Escuela Hospital had a burn unit directed by Dr. César Enríquez, a plastic surgeon. The unit had been in operation for about ten years. Carlos remembers I murmured: "Carlos, the doctors are taking good care of us. Let's stay here." I said this because I felt like I was dying, and I didn't want to be moved even slightly.

Dr. Del Carmen left the hospital exhausted and went home. My parents loved him like a son, and thanks to him, we had quality care while we were at Escuela Hospital in Honduras. That is why we will always keep him in our hearts. And why wouldn't we, since he was with us in those first moments when we were fighting to tear our lives away from death?

Night was falling over Tegucigalpa. There were still a few hours left before that tragic day came to an end.

CHAPTER 7

"They Are Alive!"

The suffering during the hours of uncertainty following the accident moved my family by inertia.

The weight of reality struck all of us so hard it was difficult to maintain our sanity. Even so, my mother sheathed herself with strength to become the source of support that kept me going in the darkest moments of my ordeal.

After the accident, the calls to my parents' house were made quickly. Dad, in turn, tried to call Managua to tell my in-laws, Nena and Alfredo Pellas, about the terrible news, but he was unable to speak to them.

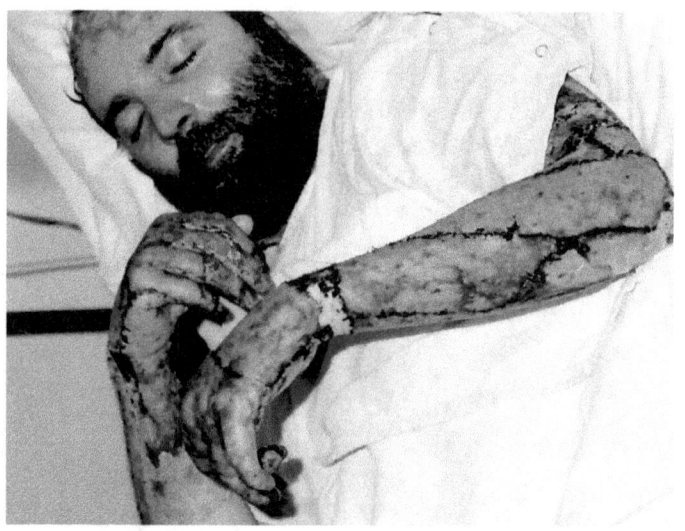

Carlos Pellas at Mercy Hospital. Miami, Florida, 1989.

At that time, my children were in Miami with my grandmothers and their two nannies, Luz María and Mina, who were like part of the family.

My brother Alejandro was living in Miami. As soon as he heard about our accident, he felt his world was coming apart. He was asleep when the phone rang. My aunt Lidia, on the other end of the line, gave him the news. He almost died of a heart attack when he heard that the plane had crashed and that we were dead. Then he thought, "She's my only sister. How can they tell me she's dead?" He put down the phone and panicked. He called Honduras, and after several attempts, he got through to Maura, the maid who was like family, who confirmed that we were still alive.

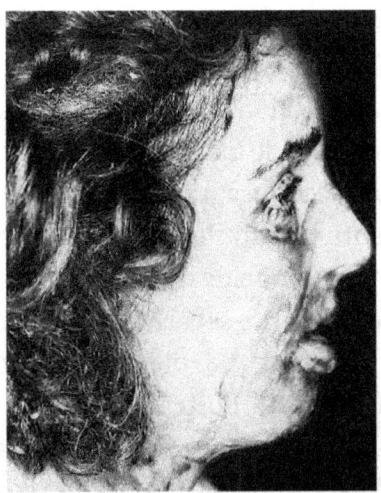

Vivian after several surgical interventions a few months after the accident. Miami, Florida, 1989.

Our dear friend Carlos Reynaldo Lacayo, who would start listening to the radio at 5:00 a.m., heard the news first in Managua. He told my in-laws about the accident, and they hoped we would be among the survivors.

My dad persisted in calling my in-laws, and they finally responded. Doña Nena was the one who took the call: "They're alive, Nena, they're alive!" he anticipated before my mother-in-law could utter a word. Right away, she told the news to Don Alfredo, who found it more difficult to come out of his state of shock.

Carlos's siblings were the next ones to contact my father to learn about the situation and offer their support.

Two family friends, Carlos Reynaldo and César Augusto Lacayo, demonstrated their unconditional support. They gave us invaluable assistance in the logistics of maintaining communication between Tegucigalpa and Managua while it was necessary since Carlos Reynaldo had a telephone with a speaker, which was a sensation at the time.

My parents had to deal with all the needs that arose while we were being treated at Escuela Hospital.

Carlos, despite the severity of his condition, said to my father, "Don Pepe, please get us out of here. We urgently need to be transferred to the United States. Get an air ambulance to take us to a hospital in Miami." My dad responded to Carlos's request and got right on it to make it happen.

In Miami, Alberto Chamorro, Carlos's uncle, covered all the expenses. I feel special affection for him and immense gratitude because he was always looking after us. He never left us alone.

Carlos Reynaldo contacted Dr. Reyna, the doctor who finally managed to coordinate all the logistics of the plane transfer. Carlos Reynaldo even asked Dr. Reyna to travel in the air ambulance to assist us on the way. Dr. Reyna's only condition was no one could question his decisions since he knew very well how medical services worked in the United States.

Another adverse circumstance arose and was now indirectly affecting us. An earthquake struck the San Francisco Bay Area on October 17, 1989, leaving 62 dead, 3,756 injured, and over 12,000 people homeless, and most of the relief services were being used to transfer victims to different hospitals in the United States.

Dr. Reyna contacted an air ambulance company. One of his requirements was that Carlos and I had to be taken out together. The plane had to be large enough for both of us, and it had to be able to fly above commercial air traffic and turbulence. A significant amount of time during the day was spent trying to find one of these airplanes. The rush had to do with finding an airplane before the end of the day since Toncontín International Airport did not operate at night because it lacked lighting.

Dr. Reyna agreed to come with us on the plane. We traveled with him and a nurse.

After many calls to several companies in the United States, the air ambulance, a Lear Jet, was arranged to leave for Tegucigalpa and arrive during daylight hours. Dr. Reyna, who was in the air ambulance, saw the wreckage of the plane crash and said to himself, "I would have never imagined anyone could survive this."

The next obstacle to overcome was getting new passports. We had the habit of traveling with Spanish passports. However, they were burned with all our belongings on the plane. Silvio, my brother-in-law, managed to talk to the Spanish ambassador in Nicaragua, who offered his help to process them. However, no one thought about how to send them to Tegucigalpa if we were to leave on the same day. Silvio communicated with the ambassador to complete the proceeding.

We still needed a U.S. visa. They took the photos from my mom's album and gave them to the Spanish and American embassies. Colonel Luis Orlando Rodríguez, an American military officer of Cuban origin and a friend of my father, helped with the proceedings in Tegucigalpa. He personally went to both embassies and made all the arrangements in less than two hours.

Two additional procedures were needed to complete the plan that would finally get us out of Escuela Hospital: the first was to get an ambulance to take us to the airport, and the second was to get permission for the aircraft to land and take off from Toncontín International Airport. All of this before sunset.

Securing an ambulance was the most implausible thing in this entire story. The hospital did not have enough appropriate vehicles to transfer severe burn patients because all the ambulances had been used to move bodies to the morgue and thus presented a risk of serious infection.

Friends and family members mobilized to find an ambulance in Tegucigalpa. Not carrying out the evacuation plan because we couldn't get something as common and simple as an ambulance wasn't possible! The hospital's ambulances were in deplorable condition. I felt sad just looking at them. Miraculously, we had been saved from the impact and explosions of the airplane, so now we shouldn't have to die from getting an infection in an ambulance. It was ridiculous but a real concern.

"THEY ARE ALIVE!"

Among a number of institutions that were contacted, the ambulance that presented the least trouble was a very old olive green, American army ambulance, which, although not a rescue ambulance, offered better conditions for the transfer. It was washed and disinfected with special solutions, and Colonel Rodríguez's wife, Marita, got sterile sheets and disposable stretchers from the military. My parents and Dr. Edmundo del Carmen accompanied us.

The air ambulance landed in Tegucigalpa at five in the afternoon. Everyone involved had to accelerate the procedures before nightfall because the runway was not illuminated, making it impossible to leave.

The last unexpected hitch occurred when Carlos boarded the plane. They had to maneuver him carefully, given his delicate condition. However, they couldn't turn the stretcher without moving him too much. Finally, they managed to get him onto the plane through the emergency window. Dr. Del Carmen explained the medical emergency to Dr. Reyna, who anticipated that everything would be under control. His expert medical eyes were used to seeing disturbing pictures like ours, but he couldn't hide his compassionate side as a person who understood the anguish and indescribable pain of the human body.

Without ever imagining all the time we would later need to adapt to our new life, we were about to start making our way down the path of a slow and tortuous recovery hand-in-hand with a grand master called pain.

CHAPTER 8

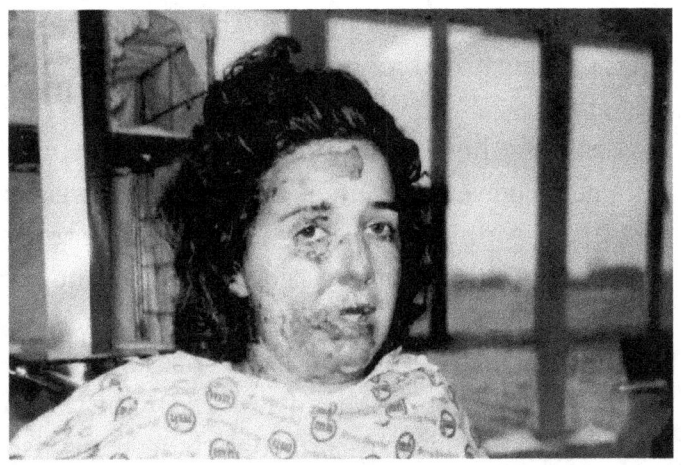

Vivian at Mercy Hospital after several surgical interventions. Miami, Florida. 1989.

"I'm Dying"

Carlos always talks about the way we learned to separate the urgent from the important. Anyone who believes happiness and money are synonyms is very much mistaken. My greatest fortune was that God gave us a second chance and that I could see my children, my husband, and my parents again.

While I was being transferred to the air ambulance, barely conscious, my dad heard me mutter some words. He put his ear close to me and heard me say, "I'm going to create a unit for burned children."

I don't believe I said it by chance. The pain and suffering of a burn are like being confined in a chamber of horrors. Going through this torture has been the most distressing experience in my entire existence.

Realizing how much those around you suffer from being powerless in the face of your pain weighs heavily on you. I didn't know if I would be strong enough to endure what I was going through, and my body seemed to scream, "No ... this is too much!"

Dr. Reyna arranged for an ambulance and a police car to wait for us at the Miami airport. On the way to the hospital, my mind was filled with deep anguish and sadness, unable to describe what had happened to us.

The immense pain was a source of endless torment and anguish over knowing my life would be foreshortened. At that moment, I had no hope. Images of every detail of my existence crowded my mind until I reached the dark tunnel where I walked with no sense of peace. I was haunted by the vision of Carlos running through the flames to save me and the faces of my children covered by a halo as bright as fire.

At times, the movements of the ambulance felt like daggers stabbing my body and jerking my collarbone out of place again. The pain was infernal. I did not wish this on anyone, least of all my little children.

The siren of the ambulance wailed on like an echo trapped in the immensity of the night.

My dad spoke to Alejandro to confirm that, in a matter of minutes, we would be transferred to Miami. Amidst a whirlwind of emotions, my brother started

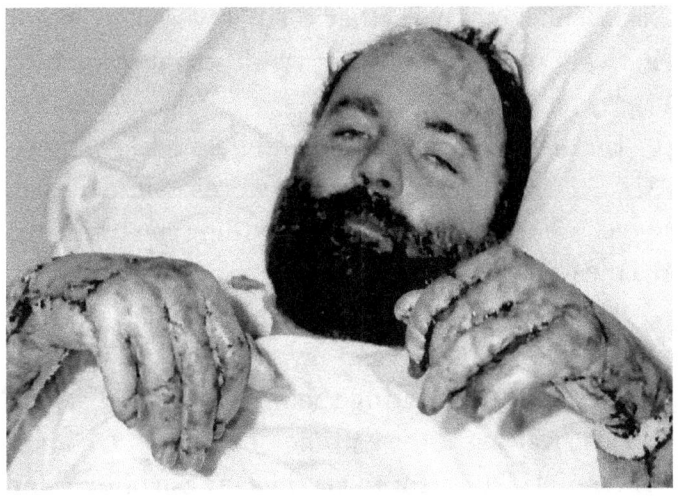

Carlos Pellas in recovery, months later at the Cedars Medical Center. Miami, Florida, 1989.

to remember our childhood, life in Cuba, horseback riding in Managua, our adolescence, and the trips to Xiloá. So many memories with his only sister! Dad asked him to wait for us with my mother, who had traveled a little earlier to receive us at Mercy Hospital.

After many hours of waiting, the plane finally arrived at 10 p.m.

Arriving at the doors of the hospital emergency ward was devastating. One of the first faces I identified was my brother's. I immediately saw the terror on his face when I was taken out of the ambulance in Miami. He didn't recognize me. Later on, he told me I looked like a monster with a disfigured, totally swollen face and a deviated jaw. Carlos's head was so big my brother would say, "What I saw was unbelievable, that was ... shocking," with that peculiar way of speaking that we Cubans have when we describe something utterly terrible.

He threw himself at me and heard me whisper, "Alex." I couldn't say any more words, while he said to me: "*Chiquita*, I'll get you everything you want, just tell me what you need ... "

The hospital staff relieved the ambulance paramedics and changed my stretcher to take me straight to the operating room. My aunt Lidia, who was also waiting at the entrance, asked the stretcher-bearers for a moment to arrange my burnt hair and give me a blessing.

Family and friends heard about the accident and kept up with our progress in several ways. Those who were able traveled to Miami, while others preferred to wait for more definite news about our recovery and visit us later.

My in-laws traveled on the night of October 22. Javier Llanes, my friend Rogelia's cousin, called her to give her the news. Rogelia went into shock. She started screaming, shaking, and repeating that she couldn't believe it. She contacted her husband so they could get on the first flight available from New York to Miami to be by my side from the first moment.

My friend Ena, in Nicaragua, read the message on the piece of paper I left with my driver, saying, "See you in December ... God willing." I also asked her to call Angelita, our home cook, to explain some details of the December dinner.

The situation was shocking news to my friends. Roberto Riguero, a friend of Carlos's, was only able to say, "I lost a brother," before he started crying. It was the first time Mariell, his wife, ever saw him in that state. They went immediately to my mother-in-law's house and found out our situation in detail.

It was Mina, one of the nannies, who remembered that Don Alfredo, my father-in-law, said to her: "Minita, Vivian is going to die," and she answered, "How can you say that to me? Let's pray to God and the Virgin." The whole family was desperate. At that point, they did not know what was going to happen with my life. I was broken inside and out. I was on the verge of death.

Dad traveled the next day to run errands related to the accident. We spent four days at Mercy Hospital. The media was pressuring the hospital administration for news about us. After a lot of insistence, the hospital organized a press conference, and Carlos authorized Dr. Reyna to hold it. He limited his participation to answering about six questions, reserving details and maintaining the privacy of our situation.

A specially prepared room was set aside to accommodate about a hundred journalists eager to get the scoop. Miami's TV channels, radio stations, and newspapers filled the hospital entrance, waiting for the signal to pounce on the doctors.

Inside the hospital, our biggest concerns were the surgical procedures and the recovery time.

There were different opinions about what treatment to follow. Carlos, in his critical condition, was not convinced by the options presented by the different doctors.

Some wanted to develop experimental practices that did not promise good results, so other options had to be explored until we were sure of what was the best. In my case, they assured me they could reconstruct my face in nine months. They would have to operate from the eyebrow upwards first. Then, three months later, they would work on the central part. Finally, three months after that, they would operate on the jaw.

Nonetheless, the scars would be horrendous since the work would imply inserting some x-shaped nails into my head to literally "hang me from the temples," given the multiple fractures in my facial bones.

At Mercy Hospital, the doctors concluded I had a broken left clavicle, over sixty facial bone fractures, and second- and third-degree burns to my face, neck, arms, hands, feet, and scalp. Also, my right eye was not visible due to a severe hematoma.

When the doctor checked me, he said, "Thank God you didn't lose your eye." Carlos had burns on 35 percent of his body. He had no fractures, but they had to amputate part of four of the fingers on his left hand.

They began our treatment with surgical cleansings. They wanted to put Carlos in experimental compression tubs with propulsion jets, something he adamantly refused. Dr. Reyna told us that although many doctors differed in their methods and there could be different opinions about handling, the important thing was that, in the end, a wise decision had to be made.

Another method that was not accepted was porcine grafting. However, the use of pig skin was medically recommended for temporary skin grafts, especially when there are severe second- and third-degree burns. That skin is placed before doing the graft in the deeply injured areas.

The benefit of porcine grafting, once it sticks, is it sterilizes the area where the final graft will be done, usually within a week, and the chances the patient's own tissue will regenerate are high. If only the patient's skin is used for the graft and then lost, it will be an issue because the donor areas on our bodies are few. On the other hand, pig skin exists in abundance for temporary purposes. In any case, everyone was deeply concerned about the differences in criteria.

While Carlos received several different opinions, and without knowing what would be best for me, I endured the ordeal of surgical cleansing.

Each day, they would scrape me three times with wire brushes and cut my thick skin with scissors. After that, they would pull it with tweezers. This process took forever.

I can clearly remember the bloody wire brush the nurse would rinse off in a bucket of water. Although the morphine dose was high, my body could no longer withstand this medieval torture. The white blood-soaked sheets made the scene more than disturbing. I begged the nurses to stop. Once, one of them replied, "One day, you will thank me." When they finished, unable to speak, I wailed, sighed, and trembled.

One of those days, under the influence of morphine, when I returned to the room where my mom was waiting for me, she said: "Vivian, what's wrong with you?" I muttered, "Nothing," but she insisted. I didn't want to tell her that, in my mind, I only saw a black hole with death in it. Telling her I felt I was going to die terrified me. I was unable to utter those words that kept repeating incessantly inside of me: "I am dying ... "

CHAPTER

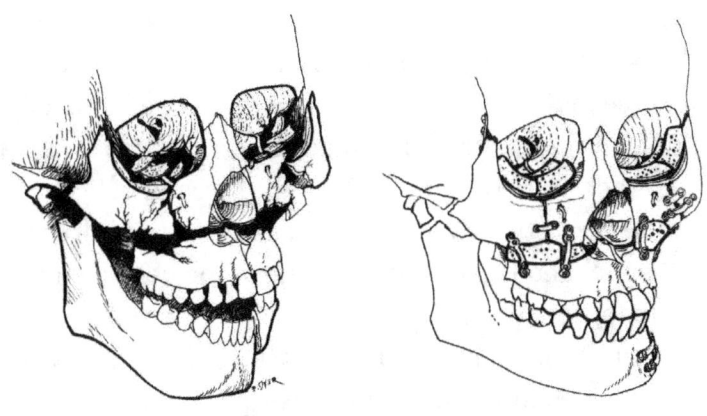

A Grand Master Called Pain

To ensure treatment started as soon as possible, my family mobilized to look for different options and opinions for our cure. A friend of my mother's, Adelayda Artime, the wife of Manuel Artime (may he rest in peace), one of the leaders of the Bay of Pigs brigade, had a daughter who went through jaw surgery under the direction of Dr. Anthony Wolfe. When she mentioned my case to the doctor, he expressed a willingness to take it on as a challenge.

Dr. Wolfe is one of the most prestigious craniomaxillofacial surgeons in the world. He graduated from Harvard University in Boston with a degree in Medicine and General Surgery. He then received a degree in Plastic Surgery from the University of Miami and took a one-year specialty course in France, where he was a disciple of Dr. Paul Tessier, the father of craniofacial surgery.

Today, Dr. Anthony Wolfe is the Director of Plastic and Reconstructive Surgery at Nicklaus Children's Hospital and is recognized as one of the best doctors in his specialty.

Dr. Wolfe accepted my case, provided I was transferred to Miami's Victoria Hospital where he had all the equipment to handle the surgeries I needed. He performed the first operations to reconstruct my face, all of them through my mouth.

The journey from Mercy to Victoria was pure torture. I felt the most excruciating pain in the world whenever they moved my body an inch. Every time the ambulance stopped or went through a pothole, I felt excruciating pain in my broken body. The nurse, noticing my ordeal, kept repeating to my mother, "We are going as slowly as we can. We are almost there."

I can't adequately describe the enormous discomfort the burns and the multiple fractures made me feel. Nowadays, I wonder how I was able to endure so much affliction. I thought, "This minute has to be better than the last." But the reality was that, with every second that passed, the pain intensified. Only my willpower, my unwavering faith in God, and the love of my parents, my children, and my husband sustained me during the difficult road I had to travel,

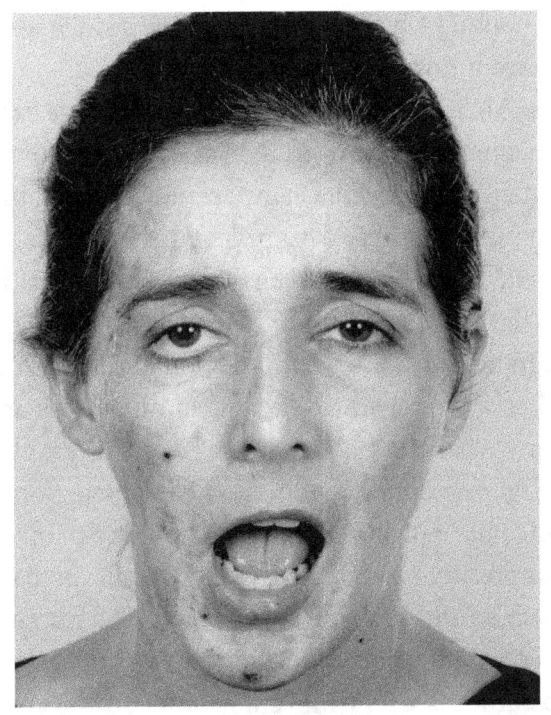

Vivian, one year after the accident.
Miami, Florida, 1990.

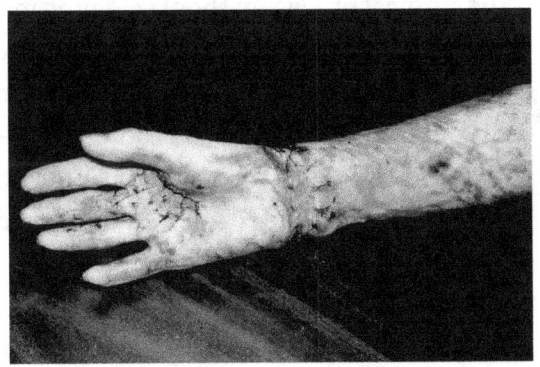

Vivian's right arm one year after the accident.
Miami, Florida, 1990.

even though I wasn't able to see Carlos since we were in different hospitals.

Dr. Wolfe had to know exactly what damage my body had sustained. The x-rays taken at the Escuela Hospital in Tegucigalpa served as a reference for designing an urgent plan of tests and exams in all dimensions.

I will never forget the morning when I was taken down to the imaging room to have my head scanned. I had to be moved to another stretcher so the device could capture my entire head. No nurse was able to hold my weakened body. After several attempts and cries, no one dared touch me. My clavicle bone was moving out of place, causing me horrible pain, and it was impossible to hold me up. They put me back on a stretcher and took me to the room. The nurses told the doctor they could not handle me since I was in great pain and every movement hurt. They couldn't help me sit up or lie down.

Dr. Wolfe emphatically told them it was impossible to start the surgical process without scanning me first. They took me back to the imaging room. Meanwhile, in the waiting room, Dr. Wolfe asked who loved me the most. Without thinking twice, my brother jumped out of his seat at the same time my father did. They walked with the doctor, who guided them quickly through their mission.

Once in front of my fragile body, they struggled to find a way to hold me down to sit in the scanner chair. I heard every sigh and choked cry and felt the shudder of the two large bodies of my father and brother. They didn't want to cause me more pain. Every movement was planned in detail. I didn't know how to hold onto their bodies because my hands and arms were completely melted, and my raw flesh was exposed.

They hadn't even touched me, and I was already making gestures of pain to stop them from moving me. I couldn't speak to them. I wanted to scream, but my mouth could barely make heart-wrenching moans. They trembled more from the tension of their muscles as they tried to hold me than from the weight of my body. They had to make a tremendous effort to measure every inch to determine where to place their hands.

Alejandro kept saying: "*Chiquita, chiquita*, don't worry, I'll hold you here or there so that it doesn't hurt." Sometimes, he spoke almost automatically, but at other times, with suffering on his face. Finally, we managed to get the scan done.

Nonetheless, the task was not over. Returning to my stretcher meant going through the same torment. We all ended up exhausted, and I whispered to Alejandro: "You can't imagine the pain I feel." Surprised by my ability to tolerate such pain, he said: "It's incredible what you can endure ... as a woman, you are very strong."

This was proof of my brother's incalculable love. I recovered the years of Alejandro's absence in those moments of care and dedication in which he protected and helped me. I deeply hope my brother will come back to me again when he reads this book.

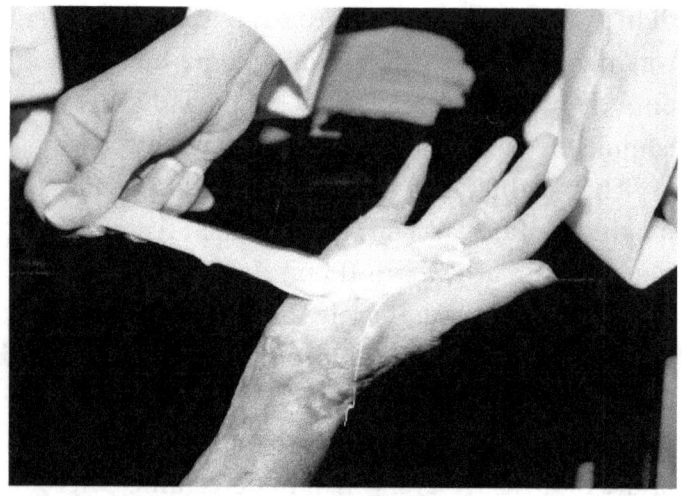

Vivian's right hand two years after the accident.
Miami, Florida, 1991.

Dr. Wolfe had to continue his work. Rebuilding my face was a huge challenge. He was used to high-risk cases, among which the most renowned ones were automobile accident patients and those with gunshot wounds to the face. He had dealt with people who lost parts of their face, nose, ears, or mouth or ended up with awful facial deformities. He had always known how to differentiate between cosmetic surgery, which only helps to correct aesthetic defects, and reconstructive surgery, which was one of the two fundamental branches of Plastic Surgery, used to repair congenital malformations, such as cleft lip and palate. The latter was his specialty and was also needed in my case.

Once Dr. Wolfe had several photographs in his hands, he did not hesitate to say I would be the same person again. My parents were in the waiting room when he arrived, visibly exhausted, after the eight hours of the first operation ended. He took his surgeon's cap off and, with an impressive tone of assurance, told them, "Your daughter will have the same face as before."

Dr. Wolfe always told me he would do everything he could for me.

My hope would now be in God, to whom I asked for strength to overcome such a hard test, and in which that grand master called pain stubbornly sculpted my spirit, preparing me for something I was not yet aware of.

CHAPTER

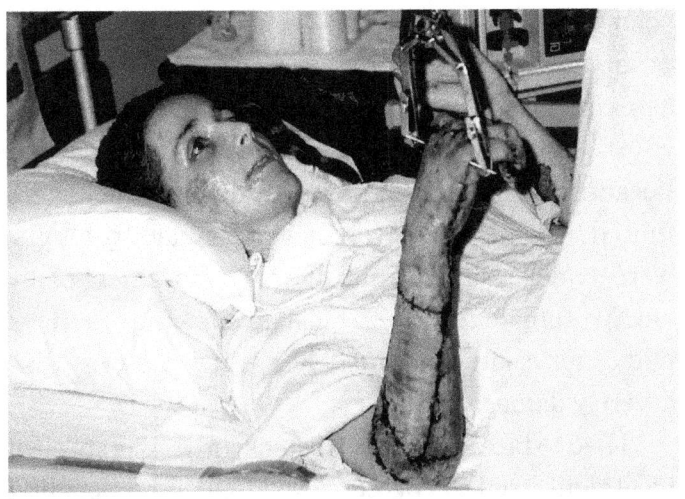

Vivian at Cedars Medical Center. Miami, Florida, 1989.

And I Stopped Crying ...

I was afraid I would enter a phase of true madness with everything I was experiencing.

I was bathed in a Hubbard tank, where they applied antiseptic solutions with lukewarm water. After that, they would cover the wounds with antibiotics. They protected my skin with gauze, petroleum jelly, and other silver sulfadiazine products used as a transitional cover because they prevent dehydration and reduce infections.

The impact I suffered when the explosion catapulted me added multiple injuries to those already caused by the airplane crash. A three-dimensional scan with high-tech equipment permitted the observation of several fractures and a more accurate assessment.

Dr. Anthony Wolfe performed many surgeries because the bones of my skull and face, which were united by joints and covered by muscular structures, were damaged and did not allow any movement of my jaw. My tongue retracted. I lost all chewing functions and other related actions. My eye cavities were also severely damaged.

I had to face a process of osteosynthesis, a surgical treatment used to correct very large and deforming fractures. To do this, they implanted different devices, including plates, which were fixed with nails, screws, wires, and other hardware. They were made of biocompatible materials, such as titanium alloys. Dr. Wolfe had to use bones from my skull to graft them onto the two orbital floors and the anterior aspect of the left jaw to complete the surgical reconstruction.

Before the procedure, the doctor explained how he was going to remove the bones. He said he would use drills and electric saws. The idea of an electric saw opening my skull simply terrified both Carlos and me.

He also explained that during the surgery, they would cut the skin until it was separated away from the bone. In the end, they would reattach it to the skull. His method was innovative. Without removing my hair, they took several chunks of my skull bones to do the grafts!

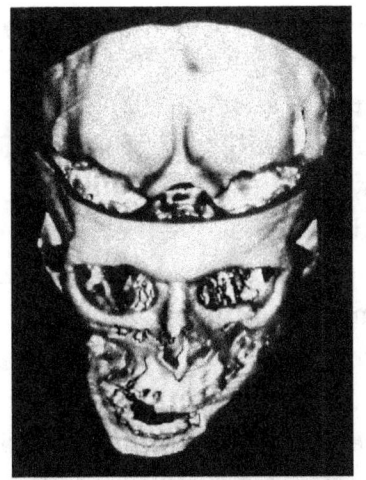
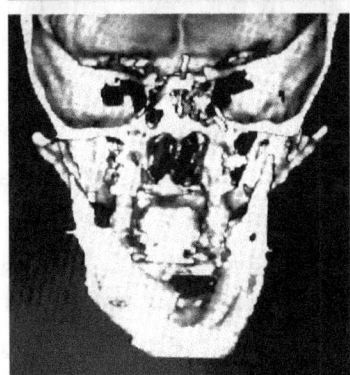
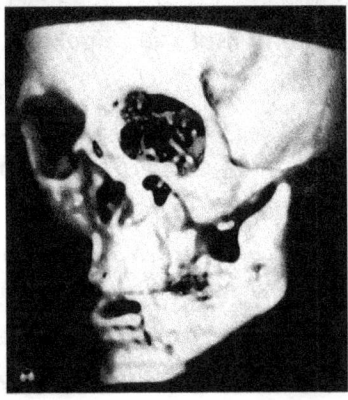

Images taken according to the instruction of Dr. Anthony Wolfe to determine Vivian's fractures. Miami, Florida, 1989.

The bones were placed in the cheekbones inside my mouth. The pain was so intense that morphine was necessary. In the operative and post-operative process, they sewed my jaw with wire, which made it difficult for me to move.

The fractures had torn away the mucosa. These and the primary bone grafts were handled with precision and the utmost care despite the presence of acute burns on my face, which hampered the insertion of implants and appliances to hold them.

The treatment was completed with an incision in my upper and eyelids in both eyes (the lateral part of an incision for blepharoplasty), another incision in the lower and upper part of the vestibular sulcus, which is formed by the mucosa that extends from the cheeks and lips to the alveolar arches, and finally, with the reduction of orbitozygomatic and cheekbone fractures, where the zygomatic bone acts as a supporting pillar between the face and the skull.

According to the doctors, it is rare to find a fracture in this part of the face, but the contusion caused by the strong blow at the moment of the impact of the plane crashing into the hill caused the fracture.

My teeth had moved as a result of the multiple fractures, so Dr. Stephen Baker had to perform several gum grafts by taking parts of the palate. Dr. Anthony Wolfe repositioned my teeth by attaching wires to them as I was eating through a tube. I lost a portion of my jawbone that could not be replaced. In sum, the bones of my skull separated from my face,

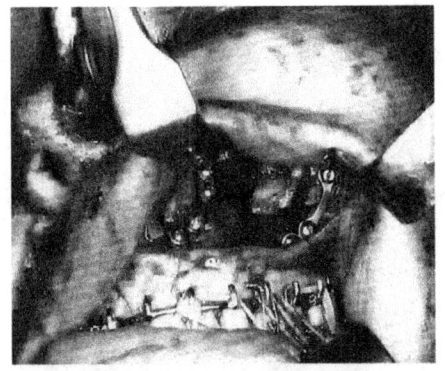
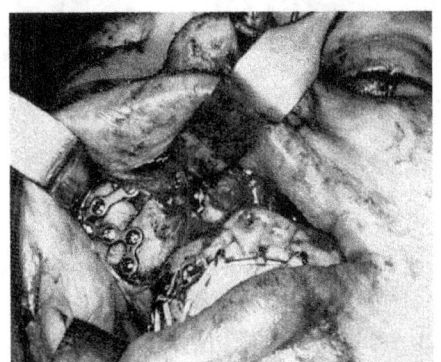
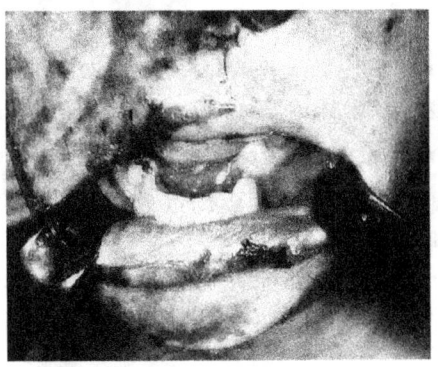

Procedure implemented for the reconstruction of Vivian's face.
Victoria Hospital. Miami, Florida, 1989.

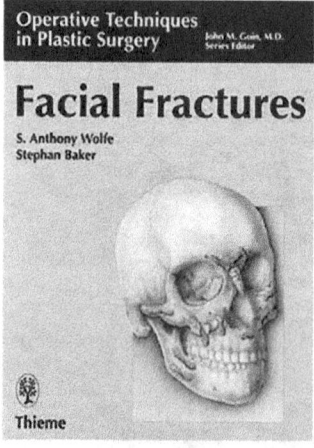

Dedication of Dr. Wolfe and cover of his book Facial Fracture, Operative Techniques in Plastic Surgery, by S. A. Wolfe and S. Baker, New York, 1993.

my eye sockets were completely shattered, and the bones of both my cheeks and jaw were broken.

Both gums were grafted. It was almost a miracle I had my jaw and could chew despite all the broken bones. I now have titanium plates, screws, and bone grafts of my skull in my face. Dr. Stephen Baker and Dr. Anthony Wolfe wrote an important book about these procedures entitled *Facial Fracture, Operative Techniques in Plastic Surgery*. My case is documented in this book.[4]

My eyes had to be stitched because the orbits were destroyed. I stayed for a week with my eyes closed

---

[4] Wolfe, S. A. & Baker, S. (1993). *Facial Fractures, Operative Techniques in Plastic Surgery: Combined Mandibular / Maxillary Orbital Fractures.* New York: Thieme Medical Publishers, pp. 138–145.

because I was not supposed to blink. Both eyes were drooping posteriorly.

For three months, my mouth was tied shut with wire. I was unable to eat. I was fed through a tube instead. Furthermore, I did not move my hands, my feet, or the rest of my body. I could not call the intensive care nurses because my hands could not press the emergency button.

More than twenty screws held my mouth together. For two months, I dealt with a mouth sewn with wires and continued to be fed by a tube. My friend Ana Carolina Chamorro, with a lot of patience, fed me with a syringe.

Not even morphine would reduce my pain. They injected so much of it in me that I suffered hallucinations. I was constantly delirious. I would see streets with dead people without arms and pieces of legs and hands. I would hear tortured elderly people and voices asking for help. Only by whispering I managed to ask my mother to speak to the doctors to have my morphine taken away. Her answer was, "If we take your morphine away, you may die as a result of shock because you won't be able to tolerate that much pain."

I had the idea they were going to kill me!

I became addicted to morphine, which they gradually eliminated, causing me to have tachycardia at every turn. I wanted to jump out of bed out of desperation. I began to see my mother with a distorted face. She would look at my wide-open eyes and ask me

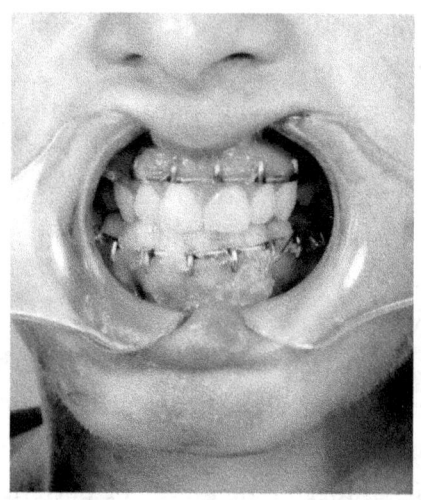

Removal of the wires that sustained Vivian's teeth without anesthesia, months after the accident. Miami, Florida, 1990.

with fear: "What's wrong with you, Vivian? Listen to me, don't look at me like that. I'm not afraid of you." Later, I understood my mother was terrified. At that moment, at the limit of pain and myself, when nothing and no one could help me, I plunged into a long silence where I was alone with God.

Cedars Medical Center assigned me to a psychiatrist, Dr. Sklaver, whose seven-foot (2.13 m) frame filled me with fear. However, for a short time, he evaluated me and treated my early traumas and, above all, my anxiety about wearing a mask. Dr. Sklaver prescribed 50 milligrams of Elavil, a strong antidepressant that partially reduced the nightmares and sleepless nights I had, during which I went into a trance and relived the moments on the plane.

In that same hospital, Carlos was in advanced recovery under the care of Dr. Felix Freshwater, a specialist in hand and foot reconstruction. Carlos had his grafts done first.

He came out with nails that pierced through the bones in his hand. I was told later his hands and arms bled while they hung at his side. They took him up through an elevator, and there he met Alejandro, who almost fainted after seeing him in such a condition.

When it was my turn to get the grafts done, Carlos asked my family not to tell me anything that was going to happen. I went into the operating room with Dr. Freshwater, and when he told me he would take the grafts from my scalp, I said in my limited way of expressing myself, and with all the wires in my mouth, "Doctor, no. I am like Samson. My strength is in my hair. If you remove it, you are going to send me to the madhouse. Take the skin from my leg but from high up because I like to wear miniskirts ... " I said this as a consolation because I really thought I was going to die.

I came out of there just like Carlos: hanging with pins piercing my hands and my feet held by some weights.

No nurse understood my pain. It was a deep pain that would not cease. It accompanied me even in my dreams! I couldn't sleep. I was still dependent on morphine. I asked for more every day. Every week, a different nurse would come to take care of me. It is very difficult to take care of a burn victim in my condition. They didn't do it right. My mother would request better care for me. I couldn't press any button. I couldn't talk because my mouth was sewn up with wires. I would ask for everything I needed by moaning.

The suffering of a burn patient is a wide spectrum that goes from desperate itching all over the body to the stinging and pounding sensations that pierce deep into the bones and flesh. In my discomfort, I felt an inner fire that seared my soul, as well as an infinite sadness.

When a person is enduring intense suffering, their mind changes radically. My personality was becoming desperate. I passed through the hands of many nurses who did not understand my critical situation. Sometime later, I understood that not all nurses are prepared to provide care to burn patients since the pain they suffer is indescribable. Only Nurse Odette Lightbourne understood what I was feeling. She was one of the angels who protected me throughout those months in that hell. She was my nurse while I was at Cedars and during the months of recovery at home as well.

More than a nurse, Odette was a friend. She was neither a psychologist nor a physical therapist, but her training had given her the enormous potential to act as both. She was capable of lavishing love under any circumstance. I overcame my darkest moments of depression and collapse thanks to my parents, who never abandoned me, to Carlos, who was always

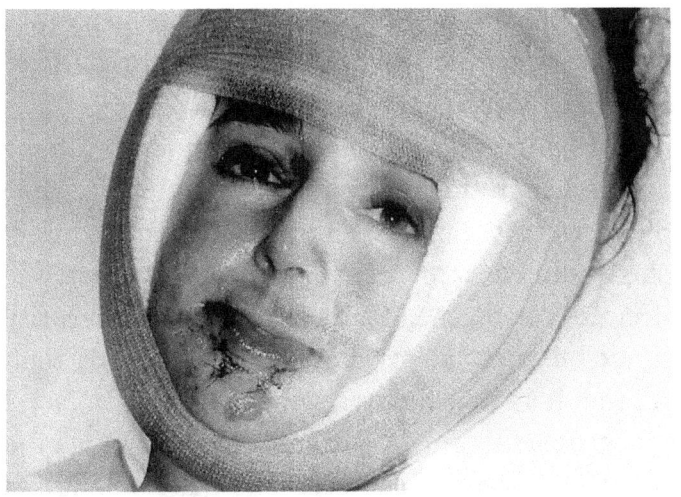

Vivian after surgery two and a half years after the accident. Miami, Florida, 1991.

looking out for me, to my children, who were my reason for continuing to live, and to her, who supported me day by day with dedication.

Odette's nursing education not only prepared her to heal physical wounds but also to face extremely complex psychological cases like mine, as well as to manage the relationship with the patient's relatives. What I admired the most about her was her sweetness and tenderness.

With Odette, I shared my faith in God. She, from her Christian Methodist religion, talked to me about many values we, as human beings, had lost. She firmly believed my accident had a purpose. As everyone else did, Odette considered that surviving the tragedy was a true miracle. Relating on a daily basis with Odette and her philosophy affirmed my thoughts on positive things. I also told Odette I would build a unit for burned children.

Two nurses took care of me. Odette was with me from seven in the morning to seven at night, while Sheila worked the night shift. When Odette arrived, she would check my vital signs. The first day, she decided to bathe me. Her decision came as a surprise to me because the previous nurses didn't do that. All the therapists did was scrape my skin. In fact, I rejected them to such an extent that one day, I saw the face of the devil on their faces. The skin scraping was very necessary but terribly painful.

Odette understood the horror and pain of touching the skin of a burned person. With great care, she would only put the hospital gown over my body after the surgical scraping was done. The only place they could inject me was above the knees.

When she assumed my care, she found bruises with yellow areas on my skin due to the ravages of the previous injections. But she would do it so gently I would not notice the punctures, and I didn't get bruised like I did with the other nurses.

The first thing she did was to replace the thick needles with thinner ones. This way, she made me realize the importance of small details as well as of being affectionate while providing care.

Odette used to talk about the strength I showed throughout my recovery, even though I always asked her for help to accelerate my healing process and to feel better. I couldn't see the damage to myself in front of a mirror because they wouldn't let me see myself. However, she and my mom made me feel like I was pretty. Sometimes, she helped me avoid the occasional pessimistic thoughts that hounded me with anecdotes from her work as a nurse.

The next day, we would repeat the strenuous routine. When she arrived, I was sleepy and in a lot of pain. At half past eight in the morning, she would take my vital signs and wipe my face. She would clean me in bed, almost without moving me and with all possible care.

The doctors would make their rounds. They took me to the therapy room three times a day, where they performed surgical scraping to advance the grafts. They gave me more morphine at every session.

Every debridement or surgical cleaning felt like being in hell. The surgical cleaning and grafting went all the way to the soles of my feet, which, as Dr. Freshwater said, was a very rare exception. Then they would put the gown on me, even if my body was still wet after I got out of the tub because they could not dry me off. After that, they would put me on the bed.

The most painful part was taking baths in the tub. My bandages were removed until my skinless flesh was exposed. They would scrape me for an hour or more. Once I was in bed, I was given all kinds of antibiotics to prevent infection and then re-bandaged. Therapy followed to avoid immobility.

The doctors described to us how a skin graft was done step by step. A dermatome, an electric device with metal blades, is used to cut the skin of the same patient (donor area) in the form of strips of different widths and thicknesses that are then placed on a plastic card and passed through a grater or skin expander, which allows it to be stretched, managing to graft the burned area covering a larger surface.

My parents rested for a few moments. They used those breaks to smoke. They needed an outlet for all the pent-up emotions they were holding back. Smoking at that time became a palliative remedy. Nevertheless, they couldn't go very far. They would sneak into a hallway, basement, or parking lot of the hospital.

My mom was steadfast in going through all this suffering with me. She always encouraged me and kept her emotions to herself as much as she could. Her presence was like a light in the darkness. She never wanted me to see her crying. Only when she was alone would she go to the hospital's chapel and weep in silence. Other times, she would go with my dad. She would leave my room at three in the morning and go up to the third floor to the cafeteria.

Weeks went by, and my mom was always waiting for my nightly calls. I would mumble, "Mommy, are you there?" She would immediately get up from the wooden chair and say, "Yes, Vivian, I'm here." She knew my need for her company. One of those days, she tried to stand up and fell down. Fatigue was dragging her down. My dad had to take her away because she couldn't withstand any more.

A couple of weeks later, I started crying. I cried and cried uncontrollably until my mom asked, "Vivian, what do you want? What's wrong? Do you want me to bring the kids to you? I'll bring them to you." At that moment, a box with notepaper with my name on it was brought into the room. My schoolmate, Azucena Moncada, sent it to me. Mom opened it and found an image of the Virgin of Guadalupe as big as the box with the phrase:

Why do you grieve and worry?
Don't you see that I, your mother, am here?

At that moment ... I stopped crying!

CHAPTER 11

Carlos Francisco, Vivian Vanessa, and Eduardo, Vivian's children. Photograph taken shortly before the accident. Miami, Florida, 1989.

"I Want to See My Children!"

One morning, I woke up with a strong desire to see my children again, despite Dr. Freshwater's instruction that hospitals were for patients.

The idea of seeing my children brought light to those dark days of my life. I couldn't hug them or kiss them, but just seeing them would be enough for me.

Three weeks passed before I could see them. My mother assured them we were fine. They were very young: Eduardo was three, Vivian Vanessa was seven, and Carlos Francisco was ten. From the start, my mom asked my grandmothers Turiana and Isidora, and Mina and Luz Marina, the house nannies, not to leave the TV on to prevent the children from watching images of the accident on the news. My grandmothers didn't know how serious our condition was, so the instruction to not turn on the television bothered them since they couldn't watch their regular soap operas.

The first one to learn the truth was Carlos Francisco, the eldest of my children. His teachers noticed he was sad, and the school principal carelessly called him into her office and showed him the newspaper with the news. She never thought about the negative impact this would have on him.

And as if it wasn't enough, they took Vivian Vanessa to her office as well, where she found Carlos Francisco crying over the news. At that moment, her reaction was to tell her brother not to worry and that they should be happy because we were alive. However, he scolded her by asking if she didn't understand that at any moment, we could die. Then they both cried. They were shocked and very confused.

When they arrived at the hospital, they first went to their father's room. My grandmothers and their nannies went in with them. Mina had dressed them very nicely. Naturally, they were excited and eager to see us. However, they didn't know what awaited them. They recognized Carlos immediately and were happy to see him. Vivian Vanessa noticed his hands were under a towel. She was curious and raised the cloth that covered them, finding his hands darkened by the burns. She was shocked to see them like that.

Then they came to my room. My grandmothers asked them to stand next to me. The first one to react was Vivian Vanessa, who cried out desperately, "That's not my mommy!" And, indeed, I was not even a shadow of the mother she knew. When she ran out, I couldn't hold back my tears. I knew the suffering I was causing my little girl.

Standing by my bed, Carlos Francisco, who was totally tense, would only say, "How are you, Mommy, how are you?" He was visibly scared. He kept repeating these words, but it was clear that seeing me in such a condition stunned him.

Eduardo, who was three years old, was carried next to me. He just stared at me. All of them had sweet but frightened looks.

In the end, they had to be taken out of the room. I was emotionally devastated. I had mixed feelings squeezed into my chest, into my mind, into my soul. I was doubly traumatized. On one hand, for the non-acceptance of my condition, and on the other, for the impression I made on my children. I was saddened they didn't recognize me. That was one of the most bitter moments I had to endure during my days of confinement. I couldn't hug them, nor could they hug me.

I spent many days depressed, lacking encouragement or optimism. I searched for the strength to go on, but nothing and no one would comfort me. Everything was darkness and gloom.

I was in hell!

CHAPTER 12

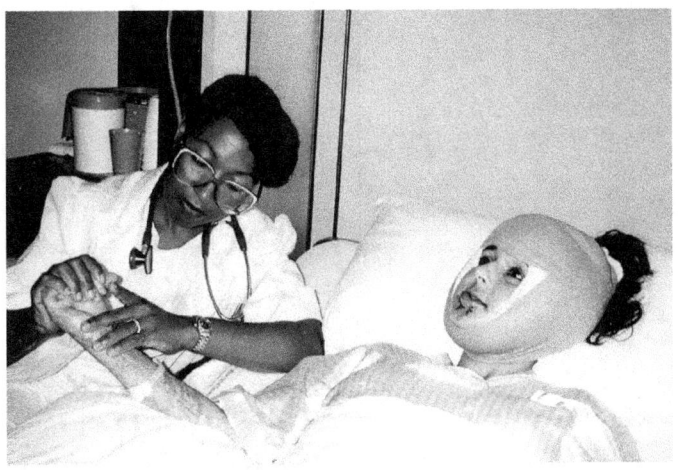

Vivian and Odette, her nurse at Cedars Medical Center. Miami, Florida, 1989.

For the Children of Nicaragua

One of those days, I woke up feeling worse than usual. I couldn't stop crying. My mother couldn't find any way to console me. At that moment, one of the nurses on duty came in to hand me an envelope. It had an image of the Virgin of Guadalupe ... another one! But this time, it came from Houston with a note wishing me a prompt recovery. Before the accident, I was scheduled for laser eye surgery to eliminate the need for wearing glasses. I was supposed to fly to Houston on October 23 to get this procedure done. Obviously, I missed the appointment!

Postcard that ophthalmologist Dora Martínez sent to Vivian two days after the accident. Houston, Texas, 1989.

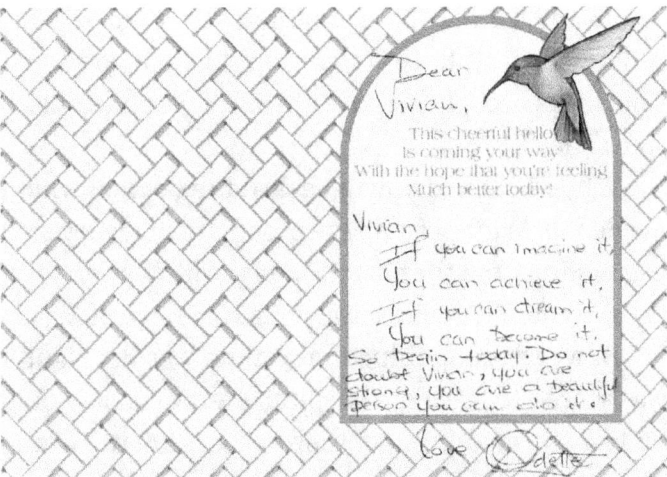

Postcard that Odette gave to Vivian during her stay at Cedars Medical Center. Miami, Florida, 1989.

I finished reading the note with great excitement. Mom and I looked at each other before she placed the image under my pillow. I suddenly felt immense comfort. I truly believed the Virgin was with me, and a great relief flooded my soul, giving me the strength to continue.

Looking for hope, I asked Odette, my nurse, if she thought I would ever walk and dance again. Before she reacted with her customary answer, I said with complete certainty, "I will do it for my children and for the children of Nicaragua." I could see her hesitating to respond as she looked at my feet, which were not looking good. She looked at my hands and arms, and all she could see were scraps of black skin with hundreds of stitches.

I kept asking for a mirror so I could see my reflection in it, but no one would give it to me. At times, this brought me to the brink of despair, and my soul ached.

When I calmed down, I asked the doctors what I needed to do to speed up the process of my recovery. I was anxious, but the hospital and the professionalism of Dr. Wolfe and Dr. Freshwater made me feel safe again.

However, something in my mind was not right. I was scared to leave the hospital. I was afraid I would be transformed into another being. I knew I would never be the same again. I asked from the bottom of my heart, "Lord, I don't want to lose my mind. Nonetheless, if that is your will, may it be the last thing I lose!"

But life continued its unstoppable course. And I realized my friends' visits were becoming more and more sporadic. Their lives continued, so one day, I said to myself, "Vivian, you have to get ahead because life goes on for everyone, and you can't stay behind."

Gladys Anderson, my mother's best friend, would come after work to visit us. But most of all, to give my parents strength. Their conversations were comforting.

At some point, my dad had to go back to Tegucigalpa to take care of his business. He always gave his all. The day he told us he had to leave, Carlos said, "Don't go, Don Pepe. Stay with us." Then Dad turned to me and said, "*Güiguita*, I'm leaving," and my answer was, "Daddy, give me a kiss … I love you very much." Those were touching moments. My dad then decided to stay.

After several weeks in the hospital, I had to not give up and gain strength to face my recovery. The first time I was lifted up was on a hydraulic bed, tied up by some sheets and seatbelts. Due to my inverted circulation caused by lying down for so many days, they tried to get me up gradually by measuring the degrees of inclination of the stretcher.

My body was itching terribly, and I was dizzy to the point of fainting. I was given ammonia to smell, and then I was laid flat again. They tried this for several days. This is how my exercise routine began and slowly brought me back to an upright position. They managed to straighten me out by carrying me because I couldn't put my feet on the floor yet.

The next day, I was seated in a wheelchair, and a Filipino physical therapist held me by the waist with some cloth to help me stand up. I looked like a hundred-year-old lady. I couldn't take a step. My mother always stayed with me. I looked at her transfigured face as she contemplated my pain.

The next day, wearing some sort of slippers made with a fine and soft sponge, I took a tiny step that caused a pain that reached my soul despite the voluminous bandage I was wearing. Several days later, I took two more steps. Walking became torture. I felt like my many scars would open up. Since my skin was full of grafts, it seemed like all my organs were coming out of my feet!

Like a child, I had to learn all the basics again. This included handling a spoon, using a brush, and getting dressed. It was just the beginning of the process of regaining the ability to stand on my own two feet. But the image of dancing again repeatedly appeared in my mind as I faced the threat of losing my right foot because the hot iron I stepped on when I got out of the plane pierced through the tissue. And now I had to deal with a scary word: amputation.

And so, I made a promise: "My God, if one day I can walk and dance again, I will do it for the children of Nicaragua."

CHAPTER 13

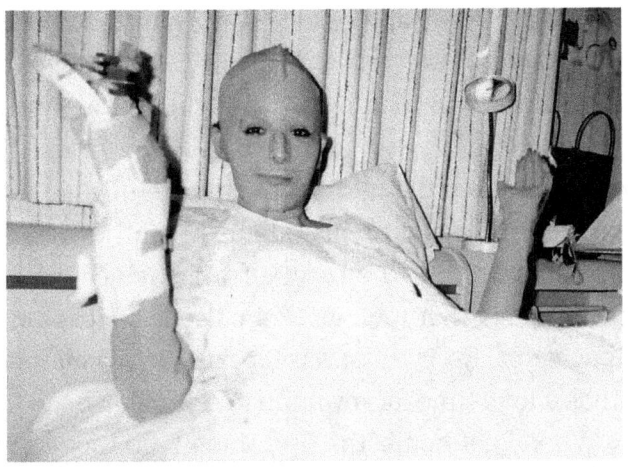

*Vivian at home, using a compression mask.
Miami, Florida, 1990.*

A Suffocating Mask

After two long months in a room, I was discharged from the Cedars Medical Center. I had mixed feelings. On one hand, I did want to go home, but on the other, I was afraid to leave the hospital. I was insecure about going home without feeling well. Even if the doctor had managed to save my foot, it still took me a lot of effort to take a couple of steps. This was my comeback to the world after the accident.

Indeed, my rehabilitation was another thing that affected my mood. In my immediate future, I had to undergo many surgeries and endless physical therapy sessions.

With unused hands and feet, the anguish of being transported in a vehicle with an airbag filled me with terror. I was horrified by the thought of it activating in the event of a crash on the road, and we would be trapped. I asked them to drive very carefully.

Every movement startled me. My mind traveled to the moment of the rescue from the accident in the old truck that took us to the Escuela Hospital in Tegucigalpa. Everything was too fresh in my memory. It took a long time for my mind to settle down.

When I got home, the first thing I did was go into the bathroom to see my face. For the first time after the accident, I looked at myself in the mirror. That was a hard blow. I was not seeing myself but someone else. That was not me. Heartbroken, I wept.

I asked my mom to take me to Dr. Wolfe to get my face fixed. "Yes, Vivian. We will do that," she said. When she took me to his office, the doctor warned me my recovery would take years ... Years? I found that statement devastating. It was too much to even imagine.

I was discharged shortly before Christmas. I have not had a sadder Christmas than that one. However, I still had mixed feelings: I was grateful we were alive, but my conditions of dependency and pain depressed me.

When I returned home, my children were more prepared to see me. Listening to their laughter and excitement brought joy to my days. They increased my faith and hope. In my absence, Mina took charge of the house. Together with my parents, the nannies took care of my children as if they were their own.

A SUFFOCATING MASK

The Christmas tree was set up with its decorations, lights, and gifts.

December 24 arrived. We all gathered at home, although it was like any other day of the year. They cooked turkey, but no one wanted to eat. It was a very difficult picture. Carlos and I were in wheelchairs. I remember everyone tried hard to cheer us up.

Starting rehabilitation outside the hospital was another stormy episode. The day after I got out of the hospital, I started wearing all the special clothing for the burned, which included a skin-colored compression mask. Inside it was a kind of mold that was supposed to shape the crease of my chin and neck, as well as the different parts of my face. I had to wear it day and night. My children were terrified to see me with the mask, so much so that they screamed and climbed on top of the bed! This was another moment of sadness, though I understood their reaction.

The mask was my prison. I was trapped, locked up, and isolated. It caused me a frightening desperation and anxiety. I never imagined that unknown world that involved wearing a mask. I wore it for two years, although I refused to wear it when I left home because I thought people would think I was going to rob a bank!

At night, I had to take 50 mg of Elavil, a strong antidepressant, because the mask didn't let me breathe or sleep well. On one occasion, Carlos took one of my Elavil pills by mistake and slept for two days. The doctors had to revive him so he could wake up.

Despite its discomfort, the mask was my salvation by preventing the formation of keloids or scar deformities. The mask, the compression stockings, and the gloves finally became part of my body. I wore them day and night on my feet, legs, arms, and face. Except for the mask, I took them off for bathing and daily rehabilitation in an area of Jackson Memorial Hospital.

It took us forty-five minutes to get to that facility. Fortunately, Odette continued to accompany me through this process. She drove the vehicle that took us to therapy every morning. The antidepressant was so strong I fell asleep on the table when the physical therapist was doing the painful hand exercises.

I would sleep like a mummy, hooded with the mask, covered with gloves, and stretched by the splints. The discomfort was exasperating. Carlos had to wear the same items except for the mask.

Every day, I forced myself into the routine of getting up early in the morning to attend my therapy sessions. I would start my mornings by removing all the special clothing. My mother would bathe me, I would eat breakfast, and then they would put my clothes back on.

When I arrived at the rehabilitation center, I proceeded to remove all the foreign material and facilitate the training. The physical therapists, always attentive to my pain, could not find any way to support me when practicing the exercises to start walking. The scars did not permit even the slightest contact with any object. Stretching my fingers became a cruel process. I would feel the slightest friction with any hard surface in the deepest fiber of my being.

After a few months, the massages with cortisone cream to diminish the unbearable itching continued in my home in Miami, with the loving hands of my mom, Odette, and Mina. I would alternate those sessions with the piano lessons I took along with my daughter so that the therapy was more bearable.

After three months, I was able to start using my left hand, which my friend Rogelia called "the miracle hand" since it was the part of my body that recovered the fastest despite being totally burned.

My parents and Mina took care of us. Mina said I didn't want to eat because of the pain. They would make me different meals, and my parents would ask Mina, "What's going on with Vivian?" Mina's answer was: "I'm going to heal her with pure blended liver extract."

One of those days, Mina watched Odette's meticulously conducted session. While Mina was cleaning, she listened to my laments because Odette was sliding her hands over my scars. She prayed for me, asking Lord Jesus to intercede for my pain and suffering.

One morning, she went beyond her prayers. She extolled her popular wisdom, which was based on the magical-religious traditions of her culture, taking a tallow candle out of her luggage, which, according to her beliefs, had healing properties through the intercession of Jesus of the Rescue. This beautiful tradition has its origin in the town of Popoyuapa, a municipality of the city of Rivas, Nicaragua, where Christ has a sanctuary.

Mina had returned to Nicaragua to participate in a religious pilgrimage to that sanctuary and to buy the famous tallow candle. She walked barefoot during the entire procession, her feet bruised, and offered a promise for my and Carlos's healing. She then returned to Miami, and with that religious fervor and the certainty that her Jesus of the Rescue would perform the miracle of healing my scars, she proceeded to rub the burns with the prudence that represented the ancient teachings of her ancestors.

I asked her if she was doing any witchcraft on me. Unwavering in her faith, she answered it was something blessed, something sacred.

Thus, her immense faith also nourished mine. I trusted every day that if a divine miracle had already saved us, there was clearly a purpose of the Lord in that fact. I was starting to feel assured I was destined to live.

CHAPTER 14

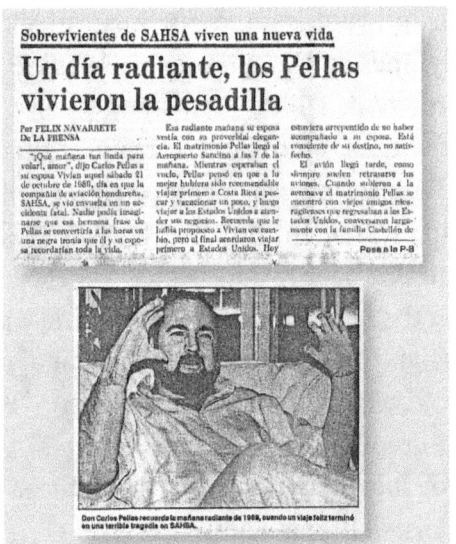

The Tortuous Legal Path

In the middle of all of this, and forced by legal reasons, my husband and I had to face the cruel reality of talking about the tragedy. We filed a lawsuit against TAN SAHSA, demanding they take responsibility, but it was never our intention to go through a long and tedious trial. We preferred to reach a settlement, as indeed we did, because logically, everything was against the airline, and the conclusion was that a bad settlement was better than a good lawsuit.

Speaking about the tragedy again, now in front of a large group of twenty-five lawyers, who were members of a firm that specialized in aviation accidents and represented our insurance company, inevitably opened the chapter we wanted to close. On November 9, 1990, Carlos and I were called to provide a witness statement in front of this group of experts. We had to wear formal attire. I would try to sit, wounds still open, and wonder why we had been involved in this harrowing event.

One of the lawyers asked me, holding a picture of me in his hand and presenting it in front of me:

"Tell me, when was this photo taken?" "Before the accident," I replied.

"Do you look like the one in the picture?"

"No," I said emphatically.

"Are you sure you don't look like that?"

I again insisted I didn't look like her. Admitting this hurt me the most at that moment.

Every question brought back the panic I had experienced inside the plane wreckage. Hypnotically, I gave detailed answers to the questions about the abilities I had lost. Each answer was enveloped in deep sadness as I realized how my life had been curtailed. I had to talk about everything I stopped doing as a result of the accident.

It was painful to externalize that my life had taken a major turn. The accident produced a series of physical obstacles I was able to overcome long after, thanks to my perseverance and commitment during the two and a half years in which I underwent physical rehabilitation treatment, which has continued indefinitely and even to this day.

The first years of recovery were a hard test to prove what a human being can achieve with willpower, determination, perseverance, and faith in God. With a lump in my throat, in front of the panel of experts sitting comfortably around a large conference table, I explained how I could not open my hands now, nor move my wrists, and that the permanent pain in my feet, hands, arms, and face kept me almost paralyzed. In addition, I told them one part of my body had lost its sensitivity.

I had to go back to the terrible days of hospitalization, tell them how all my teeth moved, and how the doctor had to put them in place by tying them with wires. I told them that over sixty bones in my face were broken and that the bones of my skull were separated from my face.

I told them I had lost both of my cheekbones as well as the bones of my jaw. I mentioned they had to rebuild my two gums. I explained that part of my face had bone grafts from my skull and was held in place by titanium plates and screws in my jaw as well as the fact that my mouth was held in place by twenty screws.

In other words, I described my torturous path again.

I can still remember that Carlos, before I went into surgery to obtain the bone grafts from my skull, told me, "Sweetheart, don't get the surgery. You still have time." I answered, "Carlos, how can you say this to me as I'm about to enter the operating room?"

At that moment, a group of doctors pushed the stretcher, and I went into surgery. It was an intervention that lasted more than eighteen hours. I thought I wouldn't make it.

I told that group of lawyers that, since my sockets were destroyed, I spent more than a week without being able to open my eyes because they were stitched up. My eyes were drooping in the back, so I couldn't blink. I was unable to move my hands to press the call button, nor could I move my feet or even speak to call the nurse.

I presented everything to that group of people who, with overwhelming coldness and indifference, were only interested in finding the formula that allowed the insurance company to get by without paying.

With a trembling and sad voice, humiliated by having to explain each one of the terrible marks that the accident left on me, I told them how for years, or perhaps forever, I would have to wear gloves, compression garments, and a mask during day and night. I recounted how I woke up early in the morning, frustrated by having to use those items and anguished by the trauma.

Moreover, I said I had to take sedatives and painkillers to be able to sleep and manage the pain and suffering. I explained to them I could no longer run or wear high heels and that my life had changed radically. I was afraid to face my first trip on an airplane. When I later did, it was a total nightmare. I had to go through special therapies to overcome this trauma. I couldn't sit comfortably for long. I couldn't stand for more than ten minutes without moving. I couldn't carry any of my three children or go on vacation with them.

I couldn't drive a car either because it was difficult to hold the wheel or hit the brakes, much less ride a bicycle. I couldn't go to the beach, the parks, or the zoo. I couldn't do household chores, anything in the kitchen, or clean the garden. I lost my hobbies of painting and playing the guitar. In restaurants, I couldn't hold glasses, plates, or spoons, and the worst part was that, due to the lack of sensitivity in my face, I couldn't feel when my mouth was full of liquid or when it dripped out of the corner.

The scars were evident. I couldn't wear a bathing suit. Daily tasks such as taking a shower, drying and combing my hair, or brushing my teeth were impossible. I could do it only with my mother's help. Playing ball with my children came to an end as I could not move my hands. It made me very sad to know that, being so young, I was disfigured, and my children, who were so little, were never going to recognize their mother from before. And, of course, interrupting my love for dance and music was catastrophic for me.

I described all this to them with tears in my eyes and a faltering voice. Having to demonstrate what was so obvious was more than painful. I concluded my statement, and everyone was silent.

The interrogation took me back to everything that had been left behind at Cerro de Hula. It forced me to examine the reasons why TAN SAHSA flight 414 had not reached its final destination. I thought about all the people who died and the children who called for help, crushed and burned by the scrap metal set ablaze.

According to the final reports and after the statements of some of the surviving crew members, human error was the cause of this accident, which could have been avoided.

CHAPTER 15

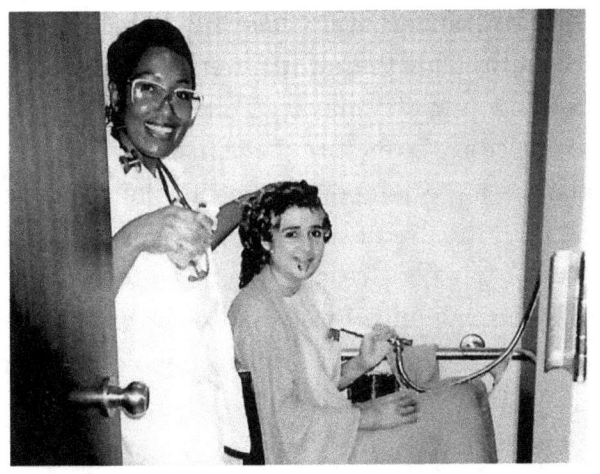

Vivian and Odette after an intervention, two years after the accident. Miami, Florida, 1991.

Life through Fire

All of a sudden, I managed to get out of the hypnotic state that the lawyers' questions had put me in. Only after the seemingly interminable session was over, I was able to return home and rest, without completely forgetting the scenes of the accident and the fear of facing, irremediably, the new reality around me.

I returned to the routine of my rehabilitation. I visited Dr. Sklaver, the psychiatrist who had treated me during my stay at Cedars Medical Center, mainly to overcome my fear of flying. When I entered the office, there was no secretary or assistant to talk to, and the atmosphere was somewhat grim. That made me run away from there and never come back!

Mom convinced me to go out on the pretext of visiting a store. To endure the pain of walking, I wore sandals with special sponges that cushioned my steps, along with the use of the compression stockings on my feet. I tried to dress my damaged body and my lifeless-looking hair. I wore loose clothing and still couldn't wear pants. In the store, people would look at me and say, "Look at that girl ... look at her feet, face, and hands." I didn't want to go anywhere. I didn't want to leave the house.

People secretly asked my mother what happened to me, and after they heard the answer, they would say, amazed, "Poor girl, how horrible it must have been to be in a plane crash." My mother tried hard not to answer them rudely, hiding her anger with a forced smile in the face of their insensitive comments. So, I had to accept the indiscretion of people who saw me with surprise. That was a difficult process. I only wanted to hide.

I began to go out hand in hand with my mother and in Odette's company. I alternated the walker with the cane to avoid forcing my body too much. Time passed, and the scars healed. Over the years, I adopted a different attitude and understood my new way of life. Soon, I would have to challenge another scenario: that of Nicaragua, that of all my friends and family who had not yet seen me.

With determination, I assumed the life that awaited me: a slow process of recovery that would continue through the years. If it had not been that way, I would not have been able to complete the social project I had decided to undertake. And it had not been a false promise made with the anguish of the moment.

Eight months after the accident, in the summer of 1990, it was time to return to Nicaragua. I was not ready for that trip. Carlos always wanted to help me break the barriers of fear and motivated me to overcome it. That's how he made me board the plane.

My parents returned to Tegucigalpa. Once again, a separation. I cried together with my mom, we hugged each other, she caressed my hair and never stopped looking at me with her light, bright, shining eyes emanating infinite kindness.

In turn, Odette had never been so emotionally involved with a patient. I made a great friend. She said I had captivated her, and I felt the same way about her. When we said goodbye after almost a year together, I told her whatever I could do for her, she should not hesitate to ask me. With the smile that had always set her apart, she answered by saying she had already received the best gift: my friendship.

Years later, I invited Odette to Nicaragua. She came with all her children to attend my daughter's wedding. It was exciting to see each other again after everything we had been through together.

The fear of flying was still latent, so I enrolled in a therapy program to manage my anxiety. American Airlines was giving a course for those who were afraid of flying in Orlando, Florida, so there I was, a year and a half after the accident, feeling vulnerable.

Aerophobia became an anxiety disorder, which, in other words, meant I had an extreme insecurity and fear of leaving my children orphaned. I had always expressed I had a fear of flying, but now it was driven to a very high level.

At the beginning of the course, the first thing they offered was statistical information, claiming that more deaths occurred in bathtubs than in airplane accidents. The theoretical classes were given in groups of ten people, mostly senior executives of large corporations, who would sit in their elegant suits and ties while the captain asked each one of them the reasons for their phobia of flying.

Each person would express their fears, agreeing on issues such as claustrophobia, take-off, landing, etc. Some of these executives explained they had even lost their jobs because of their fear of flying. Others said it had even caused them to separate from their partners. In general, all fears limit any person.

The time came for me to give my answer, and people panicked as I said my husband and I had survived an airplane crash. They turned to look at me. Their faces had nervous smiles, and I could see the surprise my testimony had caused in them.

No one imagined that right in front of their timid fear of flying, a person like me would be sharing my experience. I thought I was the weakest in the course, but the bravery of the top executives would be broken by the courage with which I related my story.

As part of the course, I was taken on an overnight flight to North Carolina that lasted three hours. This led me to incessant questions I would ask myself at several stages of my recovery, such as, *If we had crashed at night, how would we have survived?*

I worked with specialists on different techniques, including role-playing, relaxation, and breathing exercises. Some of these consisted of a mental count from one to ten, imagining each number to accomplish relaxation. This way, my attention was not focused on negative thinking.

Another technique, with unmatchable results, was tying a rubber band to my wrist or neck, so every time the airplane moved and I thought it would fall, I would stretch the rubber band and then release it, causing a whiplash. If the tension was very strong, I had to do it on my neck so that the pain diverted my thoughts.

An important recommendation was to move in the seat during airplane turbulence because the worst thing is to cling to it or sit feeling tense. We were constantly advised to think pilots are extraordinarily prepared professionals with excellent physical and psychological training. In general, they insisted we had to believe the crew was highly qualified to perform their duties.

Another argument the trainers presented to help us relinquish our fear was that airplanes are a safe means of transportation. They said that today's technology is very strong in all areas and that flight and passenger safety are reinforced.

It is widely known that there are far more car accidents than airplane accidents. It is difficult to make mistakes in airspace, which is much less congested than on land highways, where many drivers do not have the high-level credentials airline pilots are required to have. They insisted airplanes are at their best in the air and that turbulence does not bring them down, although it is unpleasant for the passengers.

These recommendations are supposed to substantially reduce passengers' fear of flying.

Generally, my mother would join me on trips, and although the recommendation was not to take any painkillers before flying, I would take sublingual Xanax, which had better results in clearing any possibility of panic on my part.

Although I did not totally overcome my fear of flying, I was more prepared to work for all the burned children in Nicaragua. I was grateful that we had experienced the accident, not our children. I was willing to dedicate all my energy to the dream I had in my heart. Could I overcome my fears and make that dream come true?

PART III

"Nothing is impossible for a determined heart because dreams come true when we have the courage to fight for them."

Vivian Pellas

CHAPTER 1

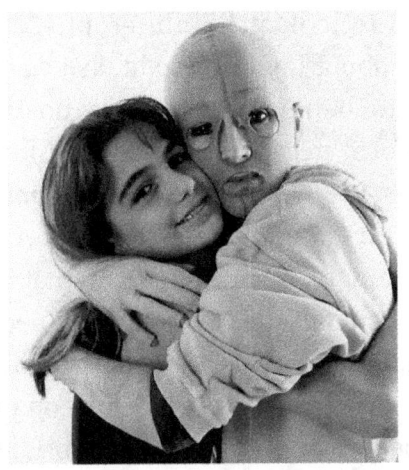

Vivian with her daughter Vivian Vanessa, two years after the accident. Managua, Nicaragua, 1991.

Back to Nicaragua

We returned to Nicaragua in 1991. From the first moment of my arrival, I decided my life would change. My motivation was to start working on the promise I made to God. I couldn't forget the words I mumbled to my father on the airport runway before being put into the air ambulance: *I'm going to create a unit for burned children.* And now, here I was ... ready to fight to make that dream come true. I was ready to bring it to fruition at any cost. God had saved our lives, and I was ready to respond to Him.

I was now able to walk, but I was still wearing the mask and compression garments on my hands and feet.

I began to look at life differently. My purpose was to talk about hope and light, as I was convinced that human beings can achieve positive things and transform negative events into life-enhancing experiences, in other words, *tears into smiles*.

After the tragic event at Cerro de Hula, I understood that every minute of life is a gift and that if you are in this world, you must be useful to other people, relieve their pain, or at least try to do so. The heavy blow I received allowed me to reflect deeply on life to find a new perspective on things and the world. It was now clear to me that *when you help others, you feel less pain*.

In my mind, I was structuring everything I could do to start fulfilling my mission. I thought the path to follow was to organize a show to raise funds since, when I was in Miami and before I returned to Nicaragua, I took private dance classes as part of my rehabilitation. The scars on my feet would often bleed when I danced, but I didn't care because my purpose was to move forward.

I could not have achieved everything on my own. The support of my children and Carlos has been key. His roles as a husband, friend, and travel companion were essential in my development as a woman and in my undertaking, which would be the most important accomplishment of my life. I had experienced the pain of burn patients and all their circumstances. I could understand and comprehend exactly what they were facing, and I was determined to change that harsh reality.

In turn, Carlos was eager to get back to work. The accident not only marked a turning point in his life but was a hard blow for him as well. He became a more sensitive man. He adopted the Buddhist phrase:

You don't learn to live until you face death.

CHAPTER 2

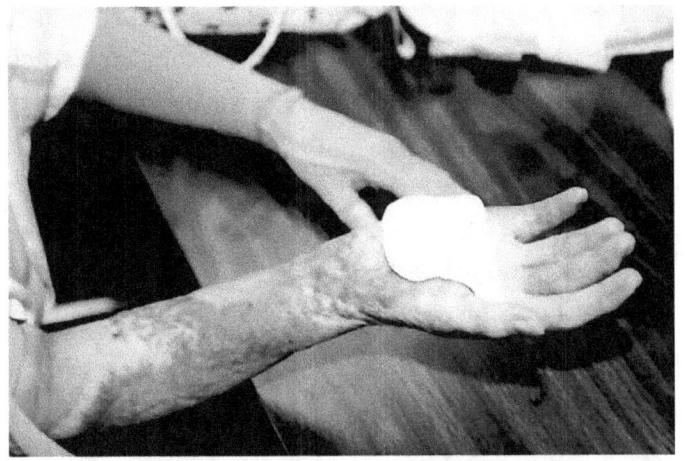

Vivian's arm and right hand, two years after the accident. Managua, Nicaragua, 1991.

Finding the True Meaning of My Life

I continued with my routine of physical therapy once a day in our home in Managua. My dance classes were part of the therapy and allowed me to continue enjoying my great passion. However, my mind kept going back and forth about why this catastrophic accident happened to us. My aim was not to find someone to blame. I simply thanked God for allowing Carlos and me to live again. I was sure there was a purpose for it, and above all, I was thankful to watch my children grow and to love and enjoy their laughter.

Deep down, my gratitude was always for the fact that it was us and not our children who had to go through the painful experience of the burns. The very thought that it could have been them horrified me. That is why I made an offer to God to create a unit for burned children.

The accident undoubtedly strengthened me in a way I did not have before: the courage to defend my ideas and follow my heart.

That's how I left my old life behind. Now, my days began to take on a dizzying pace. I had to balance completing my full recovery, taking care of my children and my husband, and implementing the purpose my mind was shaping as a "partnership." I became obsessed with the fundraising necessary to accomplish this.

In the meantime, my parents were still living in Honduras, but we were in constant communication. Every two months, they would travel to visit us as my children always enjoyed the great love of their grandparents.

It was not easy to fulfill the different roles life imposed on me and that I also wanted to undertake. But no

obstacle in my path could prevent me from achieving my goals. My burnt hand reminded me every day that I would hold it out to everyone who needed it.

CHAPTER 3

Vivian, her daughter Vivian Vanessa, and the student group of Studio Danza Ilusiones. Managua, Nicaragua, 1994.

Every Path Has Its Puddle

When I arrived in Nicaragua, I was excited to see what had been accomplished with the money Carlos and I donated to the Fernando Vélez Paiz Hospital to set up a burn unit.

But I was incredibly disappointed to find it in such dismal conditions: the walls of the operating room had gaps up to twenty inches apart at every corner that faced the street. Even a dog could get in through there! And above all, the operating table was made of concrete and bathroom tiles! This situation made me realize I needed to work very hard to remake such a substandard setting. It was urgent to have a real unit for the children.

Vivian and María de Jesús Lacayo, aproquen's first volunteer, at the Fernando Vélez Paiz Hospital. Managua, Nicaragua, 1991.

At that time, even I was struck by the fact that I always referred to the project using the word "unit." I didn't know where that word came from because in Nicaragua, people always spoke in terms of "polyclinic," "medical center," "hospital," "clinic," or "health center," but I had never heard the word "unit." I thought that was how it had to be because I was looking to build a place offering integral care where children would not have to experience what I went through during the long and painful transition of attending the different appointments for rehabilitation.

My next disappointment came when I hired an engineer to demolish part of what was there and design what was missing. I had to face many obstacles in the construction of this new space. I applied for

Surgical table at the Fernando Vélez Paiz Hospital before the construction of the new unit. Managua, Nicaragua, 1991.

a personal loan from the Banco de América Central (BAC). This money would be used for the construction of the first stage.

Multiple issues with the contractor, related to both time and money, delayed the project. I gave the first engineer I hired the money he asked me for, but after a month and a half, he vanished, taking a large part of those resources with him.

Sometime later, I hired architect Álvaro Villa, whom I grew very fond of as he completed the work satisfactorily in time and form. It was a long and difficult process that required more resources, which came from our personal equity, another loan from the bank, and from José Antonio Baltodano, who managed a foundation in New York and donated ten thousand dollars.

Procedure tub for the treatment of burns with skin scraping at the Fernando Vélez Paiz Hospital before the construction of the new unit. Managua, Nicaragua, 1991.

As I continued to develop the unit, I worked on the legal organization of the association I wanted to establish. However, my social project, as I had conceived it, would be complete if I succeeded in founding a dance school as well. And so I did. I called it Studio Danza Ilusiones to fulfill my promise to dance for the children of Nicaragua if I ever walked again. From there, my efforts were aimed at creating awareness in children and adults of the fact that dance also offers a means to help others.

My car became my mobile office, enabling me to run all the necessary errands. I worked incessantly. For a long time, I coordinated all the activities in aproquen, my foundation dedicated to helping children suffering from burns in Nicaragua, on my own. I did what an entire team does today! I would develop the publicity spots, publish newspaper ads, look for donations and sponsors, and put on the show, which meant dancing, directing the choreography and music, selling the tickets, directing the costume design, finding the cast, the set, and producing the documentary video ... everything!

People often mistakenly believe that completing a project of this magnitude is solely their accomplishment, but I am convinced God does it all. We are only instruments in his hands.

Two years before starting Studio Danza Ilusiones, I asked the owner of a dance school in Managua, where I was rehearsing, to allow me to organize a show. She agreed to it.

That was where we launched my first show: *Da un poquito de amor, da un poquito de vida*, which means "Give a Little Love, Give a Little Life." I did it despite the doubts of many people. Some of them asked me how we would go on stage when it was almost certain that no one would attend the event.

In spite of it all, I kept going. I rented the Rubén Darío National Theater, and the result was wonderful. Before my eyes was a crowd that packed the hall. They watched the show standing or sitting on the floor because the 1,200 seats in the theater were all occupied! Additional chairs had to be set up, and there were still people standing.

I called the second show *Después de todo ... es un mundo pequeño*, which means "After All ... It's a Small

Corridors of the Fernando Vélez Paiz Hospital before the construction of the new unit. Managua, Nicaragua, 1991.

World." We launched it in the same school, and it was a total success. We filled the Rubén Darío National Theater again!

At that moment, I decided since my project was not short-term, I had to build a studio where we could guarantee the continuity of the show, and this would be a way to thank the people who supported us with the children. Once I inaugurated it, I invited the owner of the school where we had organized the first two shows, but I was saddened when I heard her say, "I was digging my own grave." I lamented that she didn't understand this project was for the children and was not meant to be competition for anyone. The country was starting to function in a post-civil war period.

Poverty rates were high, and basic services were in ruins. I wanted to generate a new mindset in entrepreneurs to make them feel actively engaged with the social work that I called *"Asociación Pro Niños Quemados de Nicaragua"* (Association for the Burned Children of Nicaragua) and decided to collaborate, not thinking of it as an expense but as a social and human investment in the development of the country and its spiritual greatness.

We began to seek support from private companies, public institutions, and national and international organizations to get them involved in this effort to serve others. My husband and the Pellas Group companies were the first to respond. Carlos has supported this project with determination from the very beginning and to the present. Later on, other private companies followed suit. We needed to transform everything, but we had to start from the ground up. At that time, I met with some people who also wanted to build a hospital. I explained my idea to them. Their response surprised me: they did not want a hospital with a free burn unit for poor children!

This was another source of disillusionment I had to endure as I walked the difficult path to achieve this social project. Many times, I had to crash into the wall of insensitivity and the selfishness of personal interests.

But I did not let that discourage me. The fact that I already had sponsors raised my enthusiasm, and I began to work harder. I knew great things cost money, and I was determined to give my one hundred percent to make this dream come true.

CHAPTER

4

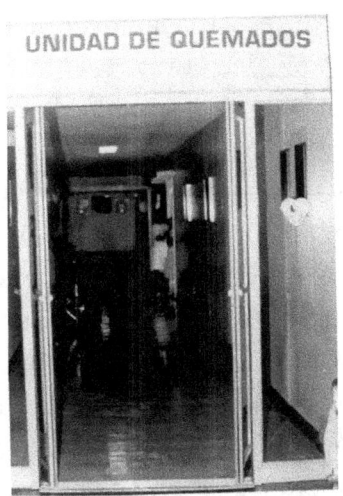

New Burn Unit aproquen. Managua, Nicaragua, 1992.

An Unexpected Answer

In addition to being our doctors, Dr. Felix Freshwater and Dr. Anthony Wolfe also poured their humanitarian dedication into the cause of helping burned children over time.

Paradoxically, as Dr. Freshwater was treating me, I was able to form an opinion about the sometimes insensitive attitude he had while fulfilling his role. He practiced his profession with firmness and severity as the only way to treat my critical burns.

His very presence inspired fear in patients, family members, and nurses alike, who would rush to leave the room as they saw him come in to treat me. His surgical procedures were almost cruel and ruthless but necessary. My dad always said he could tolerate that treatment because it produced excellent results in our recovery.

My surprise was even greater when, as I was leaving the hospital, this tough, difficult, brusque, and often insensitive doctor took me to the storage rooms of Cedars Medical Center (known today as the Jackson Memorial Hospital) to tell me, "Choose whatever you want for the burn unit you are building in Nicaragua. All of this is yours." This way, and thanks to the efforts of Dr. Felix Freshwater at the Cedars Medical Center in Miami and the Global Links Foundation in Pittsburgh, Pennsylvania, we were able to provide the necessary furnishings for our unit.

In life, you never know the true feelings of the people who cross your path, and just as I found individuals who could hurt me with their actions, I also found people who were capable of unlimited generosity, who nourished my hope to move forward.

CHAPTER 5

Vivian Pellas, President Violeta Barrios de Chamorro, and Cardinal Miguel Obando y Bravo at the inauguration of the aproquen Burn Unit. Managua, Nicaragua, 1993.

APROQUEN: The Divine Mandate!

Our aim as an association was to give a new meaning to the words philanthropy, altruism, and charity so that our efforts were not perceived as public charity but rather with a new mentality of social and humanitarian commitment. It was with this premise that the *Asociación Pro Niños Quemados de Nicaragua-aproquen* (Association for Burned Children of Nicaragua) was established, also called aproquen for short. We were only able to achieve this ambition after overcoming bureaucratic hurdles to obtain legal status and to be able to see my dream

Construction of the New aproquen Burn Unit, at the Fernando Vélez Paiz Hospital. Managua, Nicaragua, 1992.

come true. Drafting the deed and charter took nine months, and they were finally approved in 1993.

At the same time, we took on the task of remodeling and equipping the Reconstructive Surgery and Burn Center at the Fernando Vélez Paiz Hospital to provide better patient care. I remember I even helped install the floor tiles ... That's how excited I was!

The unit was inaugurated on February 21, 1993, and was attended by then-President Violeta Barrios de Chamorro and other personalities.

From the moment the construction began, and once the unit was operational, I was on site at the unit every day. And it gave me such satisfaction to see my promise fulfilled that I felt renewed with each visit. The unit and everything that was done there were a balm for my life that filled me with infinite joy. No one had seen it before the inauguration but me! It was a surprise for everyone.

We had been supporting the initiative of Fundación para el Desarrollo de la Cirugía Reconstructiva en Nicaragua[5]-NICAPLAST even before the burn unit became operational. Free operations were performed in the city of León, where there was no care to correct congenital malformations such as cleft lip and palate, as well as the aftereffects of burns and trauma.

However, the main objective of nicaplast was to offer training to Nicaraguan reconstructive surgeons through days of on-site medical work. The project was carried out through an exchange program with doctors and professors from the University of Wisconsin, Eduplast, and the Universidad Nacional Autónoma de Nicaragua[6] (UNAN–León) with the support of groups and organizations from Switzerland and aproquen.

In this way, the first postgraduate degree in the specialty of Plastic and Reconstructive Surgery was created at the UNAN-León to train the first doctors in this area, who included Dr. Gustavo Herdocia, Dr. Humberto Briceño, and Dr. Mario Pérez, our medical director and plastic and reconstructive surgeon in the Burn Unit at aproquen.

---

5 Foundation for the Development of Reconstructive Surgery in Nicaragua (NICAPLAST)
6 National Autonomous University of Nicaragua

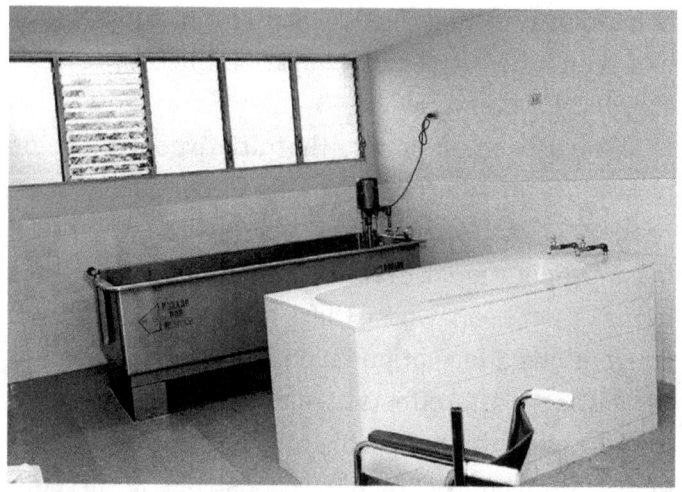

New Hubbard tanks for the scraping process of burn victims at the Fernando Vélez Paiz Hospital. Managua, Nicaragua, 1993.

As our medical director, Dr. Pérez has been a central pillar with his sensitivity, humility, and great humanity. He has been fully committed to treating burned children and cleft lip and palate. He is a true professional who honors his oath by fulfilling the work he has assumed with dedication and heart.

I intended to go beyond hospital walls and to serve the people in their own environments because the lack of information and all the difficulties of not having enough money and access to means of transportation prevented people from getting the healthcare they needed. This, in particular, was the case of those affected by the scourge of burns who traveled to nearby rural hospitals where we installed operating rooms, far from the cities. Therefore, our relationship with Dr. Michael Carstens, a prominent maxillofacial plastic surgeon and member of interplast—today known as Resurge International, the largest volunteer organization of plastic surgeons in the world—was pivotal. We forged an alliance with him to develop our program, offering free days of medical attention in locations that were far from the capital.

With the collaboration of several organizations (cited at the end of this book), we have coordinated 202 days of medical attention throughout the country to date.

The accident made me aware of the complex universe of burns, and from my condition as a burn victim, I understood the immense work ahead of me.

Accidental burns have become a public health crisis: it is the second most common cause of death by accident, and more children die annually from burns than from HIV/AIDS and malaria combined, according to Resurge International.

APROQUEN data shows that the vast majority of victims of accidental burns are children, and of these, 90% occur at home, usually in the kitchen (53%) or at home in backyards (25%) from garbage burning. Mothers are present 75% of the time during these types of accidents.

By sharing the stories of thousands of children who suffered burns in deplorable conditions in remote communities, where they had been marginalized as human beings by society, we touched the hearts of many Nicaraguans. Their burns were conditioned by a social, educational, cultural, economic, and human context typical of a developing country.

I was bringing that desire I expressed to my father to life: to build a burn unit. On a personal level, my dedication to the organization, day and night, denied me the possibility of spending more time at home. That was the sacrifice. And that's what the second chance to live was all about. That's what the Supreme Being meant by choosing me as a survivor of that devastating and Dantean Flight 414.

Every day, I set a goal for myself, and every night, I fell asleep thinking about doubling my energies to ease the pain of thousands of children who, like me, were feeling the horror of a severe burn. Walking into the burn unit and seeing our progress made me forget my physical problems and constantly energized me.

That's how this mission was born. We continued to learn, adapt, and grow, and our social work was bearing fruit.

Building a unit for burned children was God's will!

CHAPTER 6

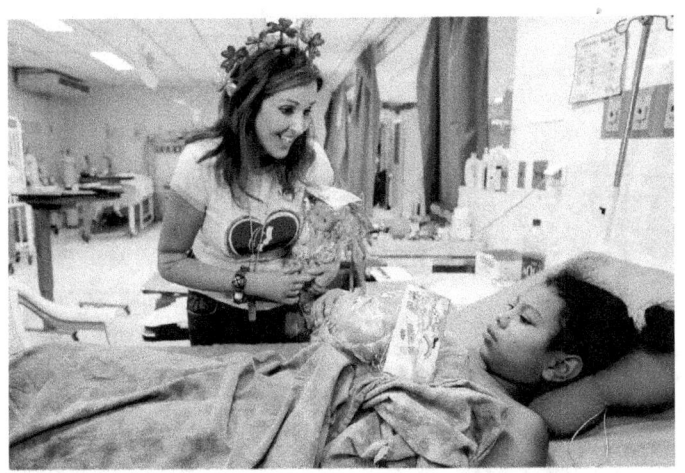

Vivian delivering toys to hospitals in Nicaragua as part of the Christmas Caravan program. Managua, Nicaragua, 2015.

Not Expecting Anything in Return

Every day, I would repeat this phrase to myself: *when you help others, you feel less pain*. This is how I learned to mitigate my own pain, and I wanted to share this "formula" with everyone who was willing to listen.

We managed to assemble a multidisciplinary team, which played a decisive role in the organization we were setting up to care for burn patients using an integral approach.

As for aproquen's purpose of achieving excellence and becoming an organization capable of carrying out a social project of this magnitude, the humanity

and humility of some doctors had greater weight than the material limitations of the space of the Fernando Vélez Paiz Hospital.

After one of the days of medical attention organized by APROQUEN, one of the Nicaraguan doctors at the Fernando Vélez Paiz Hospital, who had another agenda, tried to undermine the program by claiming that the groups of doctors who came from abroad "went on a safari" during the sessions. Soon after, the front pages of the newspapers *El Nuevo Diario* and *Diario Barricada* on March 6, 1996, published inflammatory statements, such as: "The results [of treatment] were disastrous and terribly harmful, with serious and permanent consequences due to the surgical incapacity of the participants."

NOT EXPECTING ANYTHING IN RETURN

Faced with such blatant falsehood, I immediately held a press conference with the hospital director and other officials from the Ministry of Health to inform the public about the reality. On March 9, the same newspapers published my statements defending our project. The newspaper *La Prensa* did the same on March 11.

I was reluctant to go to the unit due to the attitude of that one particular doctor, who, unscrupulously, wanted to profit from the burn unit we had built.

As I was speaking at the conference, the director of the Fernando Vélez Paiz Hospital passed me a little slip of paper that said, "Stop talking." That paper made me so angry I resolutely continued. Then I ended my statement by declaring, "As long as I live and APROQUEN exists, all the burned children in Nicaragua will receive care free of charge."

There was a long silence, and I finished the press conference.

There were many difficult experiences we had to face during this time. Despite these obstacles, our greatest satisfaction always came from providing care to the hundreds of children who arrived at the unit and giving them our full compassion and understanding. In order to reach the desired level of quality, we needed to build our own space. To achieve a world-class unit, we had to leave the Fernando Vélez Paiz Hospital, the institution that hosted us for eleven years, despite its multiple limitations, just as any other public health center.

God was with us. The divine command I received was on the move. The decisive support we received from many individuals and companies was greater than the disengagement of some public institutions that did not fulfill their promises after expressing commitment to our cause.

CHAPTER 7

Vivian in her office with the image of the Virgin of Guadalupe sent by the Archbishop of Mexico. Managua, Nicaragua, 1994.

A Queen Arrives from Mexico

Life continued its course amidst difficult and rewarding times. Day by day, with constant effort, the unit for burned children and the dance studio became firmly established. The setbacks I faced saddened me, but I never gave up.

The avalanche of help I received from specialized doctors, artists, businesspeople, friends, and volunteers allowed aproquen to remain alive. A visit from the well-known Mexican actor Julio Alemán, a leading personality in film, theater, and soap operas in his country, accompanied by actor César Sobrevals, was a timely endorsement for the organization. His

*Vivian, Julio Alemán, and César Sobrevals.
Managua, Nicaragua, 1994.*

presence alone said a lot, but what spoke even more was the gift he brought us on behalf of the Archbishop of Mexico: a beautiful image of the Virgin of Guadalupe, whom Pope John Paul II would call the Queen of Mexico and Empress of America.

It was the third time the Virgin appeared before me. On the two previous occasions, she did so at the most difficult moments of my convalescence at Cedars Medical Center in Miami.

This new "encounter" led me to a moment of great reflection as I tried to properly understand what to many might seem to be nothing more than a mere coincidence, but for me, it was an authentic message of the Virgin's presence in my life. I thought with great fervor about the meaning of the religious syncretism of the Virgin of Guadalupe to the great Mexican people, as well as her appearance in 1531 before Juan Diego, a humble native from Mexico, on Tepeyac Hill.

To this day, I cherish this image with absolute devotion and feel that it's She who has always taken care of us. I believe She is the protectress of the burned children and of everyone in aproquen.

In an inexplicable way, the Virgin of Guadalupe repeatedly reappeared in my life. And that would not be the last time ...

CHAPTER 8

*Inauguration of the Vivian Pellas Hospital.
Managua, Nicaragua, 2004.**

A Dream Come True

In my opening speech at the show we organized in 1995, I announced to the public that I was going to build a private hospital with a special unit for burned children as well as a chapel in the middle of it. I repeated the same thing year after year until one day, my dad advised me not to mention it in public anymore since I had not made it happen. I told him not to worry, that Nicaragua was going to have a hospital and an excellent Burn Unit; of that I was sure.

---

*In the photo, from left to right: engineer Gilberto Guzmán; José Antonio Alvarado, Minister of Health; Carlos Pellas, President of the Pellas Group; engineer Enrique Bolaños Gueier, President of the Republic of Nicaragua; Vivian Pellas; Cardinal Miguel Obando y Bravo; and Pablo Ayón.

APROQUEN'S medical and administrative team.
Managua, Nicaragua, 2018.

Fabián Medina published this promise in 2002 in his book *Secretos de Confesión*, which brings together the best interviews he has ever done, including mine, which took place years ago:

"This hospital has cost us a lot. And it's still costing us. But I ask Nicaragua not to abandon us and to support us. Things like this take time, but this hospital and this burn unit will become a reality. This is my promise to Nicaragua ... "

And so, we built our own Burn Unit, which was part of the Vivian Pellas Hospital. The President of the Republic, engineer Enrique Bolaños, was present at the inaugural event in which this dream came true in May 2004. I kept my promise. I fulfilled my commitment to God and Nicaragua. I kept my

From left to right: Donald Wagner, DV, Barbara Rose, Barbara Heilman, and Dorit Aaron. Managua, Nicaragua, 2006.

promise. I could not have accomplished this without Carlos's help.

We created a unit to meet all the needs that a burn patient requires under a single roof. Now, not only do we provide care for burn patients but also for children with congenital cleft lip and cleft palate malformations. Our commitment has been and continues to be to integrally serve these children free of charge from birth to the age of eighteen when they get their braces.

At the APROQUEN burn center/hospital, the patient will find a range of comprehensive care services provided by an interdisciplinary team that includes the following professionals: reconstructive plastic surgeons, pediatricians, infectious disease specialists, nutritionists, physical therapists, psychologists, speech therapists, orthodontists, pediatric dentists, and nurses. In addition, we offer accommodation for a family member and provide food, clothing, and transportation since, most of the time, the children come from remote locations and lack economic resources.

My vision to provide Nicaragua with a general hospital with world-class standards was complemented by the idea to build a free-of-charge burn unit attached to the hospital for the convenience of on-site support services that a center of this type offers, such as laboratory, imaging, nutrition, and laundry. Even in the United States, general hospitals often outsource these services due to the high costs involved.

With my husband's help, we invited a group of doctors and businessmen to become part of this project. They eventually decided to invest in the private hospital to improve and seek excellence in healthcare in Nicaragua. Donald Wagner, a consultant of Memorial Hermann Health System in Houston, was instrumental in the creation of the organization's statutes, regulations of the medical team, administrative processes, and management. He donated his time as a gesture of his humanity and commitment to the work we were doing in the Unit.

Thanks to our enterprising character, the hard work of all the personnel, and the positive results obtained by providing free care to thousands of children, APROQUEN'S image has been consolidated. Annually, more than 1,100 children receive free care at the Burn Unit as participants in the Burn Program (882) and the LPH Program (223). In twenty-eight years of work, we have performed more than 605,000 health services, more than 38,000 surgeries, and around 306,000 rehabilitation sessions, all of them free of charge!

After so much effort, so many setbacks, and so much struggle, the dream I had forged with so much hope was finally coming true! It was clear to me that to keep it alive, I would have to continue working hard. Stopping was never an option. I could not be afraid to face the new challenges.

CHAPTER 9

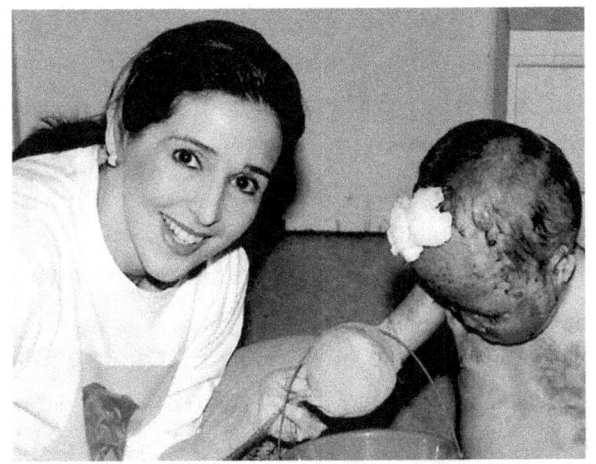

Vivian and Jimmy Rosales at the Fernando Vélez Paiz Hospital. Managua, Nicaragua, 1997.

A World of Darkness and Isolation

There have been many experiences in which each and every one of these young children has taught me incomparable lessons of love and strength in overcoming obstacles throughout all of these years at aproquen. I would never have been able to feel these emotions if it were not for them.

I have so many memories, but at this point the case of Jimmy comes to mind. At the age of three, 80% of Jimmy's body was burned. His two younger siblings died in the fire. Jimmy arrived in the unit where we took care of him. After going through several surgeries, he was still hospitalized on his birthday, and to cheer him up, we gave him some toys and a little pair of shoes. When I handed them to him, although he still couldn't speak very well, he managed to say in a soft voice: "These are for my little brother."

I was so touched to see how a child, in the critical condition he was in, was able to give to others. At that moment, he thought of his brother, not knowing he had perished in the fire.

Today, Jimmy is a 23-year-old man who has overcome his tragedy to such an extent that he became a volunteer at aproquen and is a determined spokesperson advocating the work that is carried out at the association. Along with Mareling, César, Miguel, and Freddy, among many other children who have received our care, Jimmy is an adult who is fully integrated into society.

But I have also been able to witness the harshness of the world that ignores and marginalizes these children. One of the days that broke my heart was when Jimmy turned six. We wanted to celebrate, so we took him to McDonald's. While we were waiting to be served, Dr. Ivette Icaza and I took him to the playground. When he went in there, in less than a minute, not only all the kids fled, terrified ... but also their parents!

Jimmy, Dr. Icaza, and I were left alone. I didn't know what to do in the midst of the confusion because I didn't want him to feel bad. Jimmy had come running in, excited and smiling, but once just the three of us were there, his face saddened, and he

A WORLD OF DARKNESS AND ISOLATION

didn't want to play anymore. I insisted he go ahead and do it, but when I felt his disappointment, I tried to cheer him up by inviting him back to the table to eat his hamburger. He grabbed it with his stumps because he didn't have any fingers. I tried to help him, but he insisted, "No, I can do it by myself!"

Knowing he was going through that situation hurt me, and I also realized if I didn't know how to react, much less would he. And I reproached myself for having taken him to that place. I felt bad ... and sad as well.

Still, the novelty of eating a hamburger for the first time gave Jimmy the courage to continue, overcoming the rejection, the disappointment, and the discrimination he had suffered. There were no words to explain the situation to Jimmy, but, like him, many children must face not only the trauma of their burns but also the pain caused by the cruelty of some people.

And that's how I ended a day of important lessons learned. There is no doubt the world of burns is a dark and isolated world, where the ignorance and insensitivity of people can hurt those who have already been badly injured physically and emotionally. I thought about how hard we human beings can be on those who need us most.

On several occasions, these children allowed me to see the spiritual greatness that dwells within them. There is no doubt that pain transforms and magnifies, perhaps because only in this way can we perceive human fragility after facing death and getting a second chance, where appearance matters little compared to the miracle of being alive. Even so, clearly, the lives of burned people are not easy because bitterness can flood the souls of many of them. That is why it is so important for all of us to work to transform suffering and tears into wonderful smiles and hope for every day.

CHAPTER 10

Vivian at the Telethon for the victims of Hurricane Mitch. Managua, Nicaragua, 1998.

And Love United Us ...

That morning, the rain continued to fall heavily on Nicaragua. It had been six straight days of storms.

The scenes on the evening news the night before were the prelude to the nightmares I had during my few hours of sleep. I was restless about what we were experiencing. I was sad to see how the good people of Nicaragua were suffering yet another tragedy. The inhabitants of different regions of the country were losing their homes and the few belongings they possessed, this time from the harshness of nature. The landslides swept everything away in their path.

Vivian and Danilo Lacayo, a journalist with whom she carried out the Telethon for the victims of Hurricane Mitch. Managua, Nicaragua, 1998.

Human lives were drowned in the mud with the passage of devastating Hurricane Mitch, which has been described as the second most deadly in the Atlantic, as it reached category 5, the highest possible level on the Saffir-Simpson hurricane scale! As it passed through Central America, Mitch sowed desolation and misery.

Nevertheless, what struck me the most was the realization that there was no call to action to alleviate the suffering of so many victims. We all lamented what had happened, but we remained mere observers of the pain of our own people.

And with this bitterness, I went to Studio Danza for my exercise routine. Although I didn't like to exercise on the treadmill that much, I started to walk

AND LOVE UNITED US ...

on it. Perhaps the feeling of helplessness started to transform into an idea, creating a force in my legs that increased the speed of my walking. I questioned whether the idea that my mind was shaping was reasonable or simply unfeasible, but I decided to give it a try...

I asked my assistant Xiomara Argeñal, Martín Medina, the artistic director of Studio Danza, and publicist Stefanía Félez, to join me in a meeting. Without stopping my exercise, I told them what I wanted to do. They were immediately enthusiastic about the idea. I designed my plan in three hours while I was walking!

I then contacted Octavio Sacasa, the owner of the TV station Canal 2. He took my call, and when I told him we needed to do something for our people, that aproquen wanted to promote a Telethon, and that we needed his support to achieve it, he agreed to help and invited me to the station without hesitation.

I left in a hurry. I arrived at the TV station, and in two minutes, I was on the air! I asked for solidarity for Nicaragua and talked about the help that was urgently needed for so many children, women, and men who were losing their few belongings with the tragedy and were at risk of losing their lives as well.

I invited everyone to donate to collect two million cordobas, along with food, clothing, medications, and everything else that could be useful. The idea was to unite people to give. I asked private companies and institutions to donate, even if it was not much. Anything would be welcomed.

Vivian and a child who had been affected by Hurricane Mitch at the Telethon. Managua, Nicaragua, 1998.

After this, I called President Arnoldo Alemán to ask him to participate, arguing that his presence was important. And, of course, I also reminded him to bring his donation!

And then, under the motto "LOVE UNITES US," we touched the hearts of many people, not just Nicaraguans, and the response from everyone was simply wonderful. It exceeded our expectations!

Performers, businessmen, organizations, and the fire department joined us. Bus and taxi cooperatives also got involved by transporting the donated goods to the most remote places since many victims could not be reached as the roads were totally flooded and therefore impassable.

Volunteers organizing the donations collected during the Telethon for the victims of Hurricane Mitch.
Managua, Nicaragua, 1998.

Vivian, the aproquen team, and volunteers distributing corrugated zinc sheets to the victims of Hurricane Mitch.
Managua, Nicaragua, 1998.

We raised more than a million dollars in cash and a million dollars in food, medicine, clothing, and even ambulances. We received half a million corrugated zinc sheets and delivered 250,000 of them to the Red Cross. aproquen directly delivered the other 250,000 sheets to places such as San Francisco Libre, Posoltega, Managua, and the western part of the country.

We had to stop the transmission at noon, right when we were experiencing the greatest euphoria and receiving many donations, because Canal 2 had an arrangement with Univision for twelve hours. But by that time, the goal had been surpassed!

And so, love united us ... and what seemed impossible became possible, leaving me happy for having been able to motivate and unite so many hands to bring some comfort to those who needed it most. I understood that APROQUEN had the strength to promote good deeds, that the solidarity of the Nicaraguan people is such that, united, we can achieve anything we set out to do, and that we only have to give people a chance to show they can give the best of themselves.

A hurricane came to teach us there are no limits when we work for a good cause and that all dreams can come true as long as we have the ability to dream a better world for others.

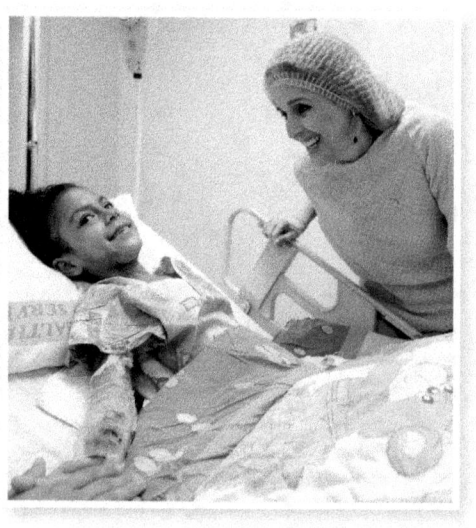

PART IV

Being a woman
makes a big difference
at work,
but I decided to assume
the commitment to say
I can and will
leave a legacy!

Vivian Pellas

CHAPTER 1

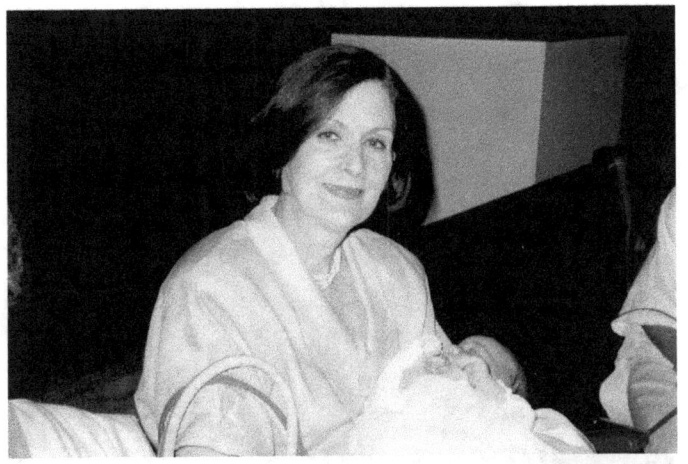

Lydia García de Fernández and her grandson Eduardo. Miami, Florida, 1986.

An Irreplaceable Human Being

Saving lives was the purpose I decided to fulfill, but now I was facing a new test: my own mother's life was coming to an end, and there was nothing I could do to stop it.

A cancer diagnosed by the end of 2003 was consuming her body, although it never defeated her spirit. The only time I felt her anguish was when the doctor coldly confirmed she only had three months to live. She picked up the phone and called me. "Vivian, Vivian! I don't want to die!" she managed to say, crying. I was obviously distressed by her despair. "Mommy, Mommy, what's going on? Why are you

Lydia García Fernández and José Fernández de la Torre, Vivian's parents. Managua, Nicaragua, 2003.

saying that?" In tears, she could barely repeat the terrible sentence she had received.

I immediately took a plane to Miami to be with her.

I know she had to endure moments of deep sadness as she saw how she was running out of time, but she still maintained that indelible strength that had always characterized her. She ... the model, the inspiration, the guiding light of my life, was now preparing for her last journey.

After I founded aproquen, my mom kept motivating me to continue dreaming. She never stopped supporting my goals. But in those days of her illness, my decision was singular: to care for her.

I wanted to be there for her in those moments of tribulation and do for her what she had done for me with so much love and always with unwavering support. That's why I suffered her pain and even had to lie to her to prevent her from worrying. I didn't want anything to upset her. So, in that autumn of her existence, I was totally dedicated to my mother. Life offered me the opportunity to return some of the abundant care I received from her, but paradoxically, it was at the end of her life when there would be no later, only a goodbye.

Facing the somber prelude to my mother's death, I resisted and tried to deny the reality. Her emotional, physical, and psychological state became my identity, to the point I felt my body merging with hers until, suddenly one day, I realized I was leaving with her. Understanding the reality, I reacted and accepted the fact that I had to let her go. I would have to find the strength to continue. I ordered my will to resist, even though I was devastated inside.

A year before her death and when my mom's health began to decline, my dad had to leave his job as a manager of the company he worked for in Tegucigalpa so he could devote all his time to her. From that moment on, he was with her and did not leave her side for one single second. He looked after her attentively day and night. He was her shadow as well as her guardian and took care of her with the same love he swore to her from the balcony of his house in Havana when he fell in love with her.

A few months later, my mother underwent one last surgery. Unfortunately, the doctors were no longer able to do anything for her due to the advanced state of her illness. Together, my father, my brother, and I decided not to tell her the surgery had failed. They asked me to come in and pretend everything was okay while they hid their tears behind the door.

"What joy, Mommy, you look so well! See? We're going to celebrate very soon!"

Mom used to read a lot about medicine, and I could tell by her expression and the way she looked at me that she understood everything very clearly and didn't believe a word I had said. Moreover, she knew me too well for me to be able to lie to her.

A few days later, my mom was dying. I was by her side, and although my voice was drowned in my tears, I was able to tell her:

"Mommy, I ask you that wherever I go, you will always be with me ... "

She gave me a deep look with her green eyes and, with a sigh, said, "Everything I'm going to miss! ... Vivian, take good care of your family ... my ballerina ... "

My dad had not left her side all that time, but a little while before her passing, he had gone out to the funeral home. I waited for him to come back, standing by the elevator, hoping it wouldn't open so I didn't have to give him the news. When he saw me, he understood she was gone.

There, part of my very being left me.

CHAPTER 2

Lydia García Fernández and José Fernández de la Torre, Vivian's parents. Managua, Nicaragua, 2003.

The Burden of Loneliness

We understand the value of time and the brevity of our existence only when we face the physical absence of the people we love. And we are left with the hope of reunion to try to cope with the sensation of vulnerability that loneliness and the absence of the departed immerse us in.

My dad was utterly crushed when my mom died on July 21, 2005. Her funeral was held on the 54th anniversary of their wedding. He mourned her like a child. He lost his wife, his faithful friend and confidant, his constant companion in adventures and exile.

Vivian with her children, accompanied by her husband, mother, and grandmother. Miami, Florida, 1986.

I was moved to see him so devastated. Carlos and my children helped me to bear such a strong emotional burden, even though they, too, were devastated.

From then on, Maura, who was part of our family and had been by my parents' side for almost fifty years, stayed with my father in Tegucigalpa. We were with him for a few days, and my son Eduardo accompanied him for a few more weeks.

My dad couldn't sleep after the funeral. He would get up and wander around the house with the terrible weight of loneliness. One night, he asked Maura for help because he felt very bad. Without knowing it, he suffered a minor heart attack.

After a few weeks of enduring my mother's death, I had to face the devastating news of my father's

Carlos Pellas and José Fernández, Vivian's father. Danlí, Honduras, 1980.

condition: he was diagnosed with colon cancer. Carlos asked him to also go for a general check-up before the surgery, and they found cancer in both of his lungs.

The doctor told us his case was rare: there were no metastases, and the three types of cancer were different. They had nothing to do with each other. This was a time of great distress that was not easy to go through.

The doctor gave him seven months to live.

Even though I was heartbroken, I had to put on a coat of armor so I wouldn't fall apart. I kept calling him to ask how he was doing, hoping to give him strength. In his typical pleasant tone, he would take my calls and say, *"Güiguita, how are you? Everything is very good here."*

We were by his side during the treatment and chemotherapy sessions at the Sylvester Comprehensive Cancer Center at the University of Miami. Once each session ended, he would not have any strength or energy to walk. At those moments, I ordered my will to be strong as I remembered my mother taking care of me, armed with an indestructible faith, and without showing a hint of distress in front of anyone.

That's how I behaved in front of my children. I didn't want to cause them any more pain. I was a lightning rod for their sadness since they had just experienced the first great loss of their lives, and it seemed they would have to prepare for the second one. This situation was extremely difficult for them because they always received such immense love from their grandparents.

They enjoyed their affection because they were *full-time grandparents* and were absolutely present at all times. They gave them the emotional support they needed and were there for all the happy moments of their childhood and teenage years. In addition to being grandparents, they assumed the role of "second parents." How would the children be able to fill the enormous void left by their departure, and how would they cope with the immense solitude that they, and all of us, would feel without them?

My dad loved Carlos as if he were his son. He would say: *"Carlos is the equivalent of four good children. If I could do something for him at any time, I would do it.*

I'm very fond of him even though I argue with him, not about pesos and centavos, but about feelings. Vivian found a partner there who respects and loves her. Carlos is a great man, a good husband."

One of those nights, I dreamed about my mother. In the dream, the phone rang, and I talked to her.

"Mommy, I can't believe it's you!" I said enthusiastically. "Well, yes, it's me."

"But Mommy, how are you calling me?" "Well, what do you think?"

"Mommy, how are you?"

"Very well, Vivian," she answered happily.

"Who are you with, Mommy?"

"With your grandmother, Isidora."

"Mommy, have you seen me?"

"Yes, I saw you the other day when you were taking a bath."

"And how do you see me?"

"I see you are well, Vivian."

Then I took an elevator to the floor above and found her lying down. Her face looked very peaceful. The dream ended without us saying goodbye. I don't know what happened. Now, every night, I wait for her to phone me again so I can talk to her and feel that she continues to enlighten me.

My mom's example made me think of a way to eternalize the meaning of her life. My parents had some financial resources that they wanted to donate to aproquen. When he gave them to me, my dad expressed his desire to dedicate this contribution to the construction of a Rehabilitation Center in memory of my mother.

I was very happy with this decision because she deserved it: she was a woman, a wife, and a mother in the true sense of the word. She was always faithful to life, hope, joy, and optimism. She would please others instead of asking for anything for herself. She would offer help instead of expecting help. She trusted in the future in spite of all adversities. I never heard a word of criticism towards anyone from her lips. She was always with me when I was in despair and endured my pain with unwavering benevolence.

Carlos had a special relationship with her. He got to know her so well he could define her through her different facets: mother-in-law, mother, wife, and grandmother. He argued that she had imprinted several common aspects on each of those roles: humility, generosity, abnegation, altruism and a great humanistic capacity, cordiality, and mercy. She never knew arrogance or selfishness. Her youthful style made everyone like her. She was concerned about the well-being of others and especially that of the family. Her only weakness was to live trying to please everyone.

CHAPTER 3

Vivian and her father during the inauguration of the Lydia Fernández Rehabilitation Center. Managua, Nicaragua, 2010.

"Here I Am ... My Ballerina"

The last thing I could say to my mom, shortly before her departure, was really a plea, *"Wherever I am, always be with me!"* I understood then that my father's proposal would fulfill that desire. That way, she would remain by my side by becoming part of one of my reasons for living, which she knew very well. Not only her name but also her presence are still alive through the Lydia Fernández Rehabilitation Center. This is how she continues to participate in this dream that she promoted and helped to create.

The Center plays a substantial part in the recovery of a burn patient, especially considering that rehabilitation reduces the surgery rate. In that space, the prodigious hands of the physical therapists become a balm for the children, who recover the movement of their body and find relief from their pain. The physical therapists accompany them from the time they are admitted until they are discharged to continue their rehabilitation at the Center.

This is a process of days, months, and years until the therapists find satisfaction in the faces of these children who are able to continue with their lives, return to their communities and municipalities, and go back to school to see their friends again.

Opening this rehabilitation center specialized in burns represented significant progress for aproquen since this was the first one of its kind in Central America and the second in Latin America. My father had the opportunity to see this work completed because, by God's grace, he lived for seven more years after his diagnosis. The treatment he received had favorable results, and, contrary to the seven-month prognosis he had been sentenced to, he was able to stay with us for a longer time.

I remember that when the doctors announced he would only live seven months, he said:

"*Güiguita*, I'm going to put all my things in your name, and I'll keep the money that I'll need for these seven months. I will transfer the rest of it to your account."

Aware that time was passing and that he was still alive, one morning he told me:

Vivian wearing aproquen's softball team jersey, standing next to her father. Managua, Nicaragua, 2011.

"Hey, *Güiguita*, it seems that the *One above* has given me more time ... I wanted to ask you if you could give me a monthly allowance to cover my expenses out of the money I gave you."
I answered:
"Dad, that money is yours. Take all of it."
But one day, the time came for my dad to leave, and grief flooded us again. Now, he and my mom live in our hearts and our memories, leaving us a legacy after walking through this world.

CHAPTER 4

Fountain in Vivian's office, where the water traced the image of the Virgin. Managua, Nicaragua, 2010.

A New Sign

One afternoon, while I was alone in my office after returning from the burn unit, I was listening to the soothing sound of a small electric fountain for several hours. The fountain had a constant flow of water and was next to my desk. On the small rectangular bronze base, which is about six inches long, small river stones are arranged, and a glass pedestal, no taller than eight inches, rises above it. The water flows from the stones and circulates upwards over the glass, cascading back to make the same journey again and again.

In my office, the lighting system is composed of small spotlights directed at the walls that discreetly and directly focus on a couple of paintings and photographs. This is how I observed the fountain when my friend Antonio Castillo and his son came to visit me. We talked for a few minutes, and when he said goodbye, he said:

"Vivian, the image of the Virgin I'm seeing is beautiful."

"Yes," I answered, "I've always had the Virgin of Guadalupe behind my back!"

He immediately answered me:

"No, I'm not talking about that one. I mean the Virgin reflected in the glass of the fountain."

I looked at the fountain and saw the image of a Virgin engraved on the glass and reflected on the wall for the first time. We examined it more closely to confirm what we were seeing. Our surprise was considerable when we saw the figure of a Virgin outlined on the glass and the wall, revealing the features of her face and her clothing. A sublime sensation washed over us. We could not believe the vision before us.

I disconnected the fountain and did not turn it on again. Months later, the image was still there, and her features were even clearer. Her presence was company for me.

The fountain is still in my office 10 years later. Sometimes, I go in thinking that one day the image won't be there since it may be a physical phenomenon that can be explained by the solidification of the minerals transferred by the water, which may be impregnated on the glass and that may disappear one day. However, the image of the Virgin remains, and my faith in her is equal to the first day she appeared.

The same year of this apparition, as a great coincidence, the Nicaraguan Association of the Knights of the Sovereign Military Order of Malta, during the celebration of the first vespers of the Nativity of the Blessed Virgin Mary on September 7, 2010, granted me the "Grand Cross Pro Merito Malitensi," a distinction and the highest honor granted to non-members of the Order or Heads of State, to promote and disseminate the image of the Virgin Mary.

The Virgin has accompanied me permanently during this beautiful social work of turning tears into smiles, sealing the role of APROQUEN as a divine mandate forever.

CHAPTER 5

*Inauguration of the Chapel of the Holy Spirit.
Managua, Nicaragua, July 7, 2016.*

And If the Fire Rages ...

Sitting in the small garden of Studio Danza, the fresh air of a sunny morning fills me with immense joy. As I contemplate the old tree and the slow fall of the yellow flowers in this serene Nicaraguan summer, the hectic days of my life come to my mind. It took almost twenty-seven years for me to fulfill another promise ... to build the Chapel of the Holy Spirit. At last, I had succeeded!

The Chapel is very beautiful. It simulates the wing of a white dove with the cross on top. My wish, which became a reality, was that from all the floors of the hospital, the patients could see the cross to remember they were not alone and would always keep their faith. Everything in it is full of symbolism: the purple color of the penitents, the light of hope, the doves suspended from the ceiling represents the Holy Spirit, and the red color represents the wine that becomes the blood of Christ.

The Chapel was inaugurated on July 7, 2016 ... twenty-seven years after the accident.

How time has passed!

My children have grown up, and I see who they are today with immense satisfaction.

Vivian Vanessa, my beloved daughter, my dance partner, and my artist, has offered me her company since she was a child. When she was born, I felt as if sugar had fallen from the sky. And I wasn't wrong because she has always walked with me with all her sweetness, even though her character was defined when she was very little!

Eduardo, with the great joy that characterizes him, has always been very affectionate and concerned for me. When he was nine months old, I told Luz Marina, his nurse, "We have to stop him from growing ... look how beautiful he is!" He looked like baby Jesus.

Carlos Francisco, my eldest son, with his great nobility—from him, I have learned so many things! As a child, he was the most restless of all. The first word he said was *hormiga*, which means "ant" in Spanish. He enjoyed fishing with his father very much. He knows I will always be there for him.

Outside view of the Chapel of the Holy Spirit, in the center of the Vivian Pellas Hospital. The structure simulates the wing of a dove. Managua, Nicaragua, 2016.

My three children were the great adoration of my parents. From childhood, they showed immense sensitivity and have been very loving to both their father and me. I never had to help them with their homework!

Vivian Vanessa and Eduardo joined their lives to two unparalleled human beings: Juan Carlos and Milena, who also became my children and an important part of our family. The best thing is they brought more joy to my world with my grandchildren: Vivian Isabella, Juan Carlos, Sienna Nicole, Nicolás, Pietro, Joaquin, Valentina, and Lorenzo. They fill our home with tenderness and love.

Curiously, my mind now evokes that phrase that I, at the age of seven, said in my prayers: *My God, if you send me something, let it be something where I can help many people.* And, well, my words have been transformed into concrete deeds!

Memories follow their whimsical parade, and now I return to the days when the road was not visible, and there was only a mountain of problems before my eyes! I would come home in the middle of the night and lie in bed, crying, begging God for a sign to go on.

Today, I have the enormous satisfaction of knowing that many have experienced the pleasure of giving and that dance can help others, just as all the people who have participated in the annual shows have. It only takes goodwill and love.

Many wonderful individuals have appeared in my life and have helped make aproquen what it is today:

Night view of the Chapel of the Holy Spirit.
Managua, Nicaragua, 2016.

Exterior view of Studio Gimnasio Ilusiones. Managua, Nicaragua, 2019.

people dedicated to a cause, working unconditionally to give a future to so many children.

Although terrible things happen in today's world, it is also true that most people are good-hearted. You just have to find them and give them the opportunity to help the less fortunate. Everyone can do a lot to support another human being from his or her own circumstances. We must help in the good times and bad times because there will always be someone less fortunate than we are. Not only can we help out economically, but also by dedicating some of our time and, above all, by giving a lot of love.

With so many negative experiences in my life, anyone might think I haven't been happy. However, it has been the complete opposite. I can say I am grateful for each and every one of my painful experiences because, through them, I found what true happiness is, and I can assure you I feel totally fulfilled. Not once, but many times, I have been comforted by being able to transform the tears of a child into a bright smile with this social enterprise that belongs to all Nicaraguans and that goes beyond borders.

Perhaps everything could have been better, but if there is something I thank God for, it is for allowing me to inspire others, especially those who have come to aproquen to stay and who, with their commitment, loyalty, and love, will continue to contribute to this social work when I am no longer in this world. That is my wish.

I want to remind the world that our pain is less when we help other people.

God has been very good to me, the same way He has surely been to each of the beings He created. My connection to Him is special, and I can never thank Him enough for allowing Carlos and me to be saved. We cannot forget that everything we do is possible with His help. We cannot lose sight of the fact that we are only instruments in His hands. I thank Him for allowing me to live, love, and dream.

I will never regret experiencing everything I have gone through. It was precisely this that led me to know another dimension of the world, of love, friendship, life, pain itself, and hope. Now, when I look back, I think all this could only have been done by God's will. Here, I'm referring to the enthusiasm, the strength, and the conviction that only He and my family could inspire in me.

I have no doubt that, through all the people who have helped us, I have known a better world.

Today, as I tell the story of my life, I feel a combination of nostalgia and joy.

I have learned we should not wait for a second opportunity on our path. I ask myself if I have taken full advantage of the one I was given and if I have fulfilled my commitment, which I expressed in that poem with hope some time ago ...

> *Child ...*
> *I will shelter you with my hair*
> *And in the air will I seek a balm that*
> *mitigates the pain*
> *And if the fire rages*
> *I will quench it with my tears.*

Did I do it right? Only time will tell.

And I look at the swaying of the yellow flowers in the grass and sigh as I think about all the work I still have to do!

Epilogue

It was inevitable that tears would fall from my eyes as I started writing this book. My mind and body relived the moments of anguish I experienced in the accident, as well as all the most traumatic episodes of my existence.

Today, several years after I started writing, I am ready for closure. Recalling everything that happened and putting it down on paper was a real catharsis. Now, I feel even more free since facing my past has allowed me to better process all the suffering I went through.

But why did I write this story? Without a doubt, my intention is to leave a testimony of how my life is a miracle, and with this, I want to tell everyone who reads it that the strength of Faith is the best shield to travel this road.

Without Faith, there is nothing.

When it inhabits you, Faith is the strength that lifts you with enough impetus to overcome any fear! Therefore, this book is also a tribute to God and the Virgin, who made herself present in multiple diverse forms during the most difficult moments of my life.

With this book, I want to inspire others to fill their lives with the greatest pleasure a human being can experience: *helping others*. What better reason to live could anyone have?

The airplane accident taught me many things and gave me, above all, enormous courage to take a "leap." It made me realize how great life is as well as how little most human beings do for others.

And in this sense, I would like to acknowledge all those who worked with me over the years to turn my dreams and plans into a reality. I have been blessed to have the support of my family as well as that of the valuable people who have been by my side, many of them since I founded APROQUEN, and others who joined me along the way.

Some very special individuals have been with me through the good times and the bad, becoming pillars of this social work. With love, time, and joy, they demonstrated their unconditional support, and this is how we managed to get to where we are today.

Many fall in love with our work and contribute with their effort to help these children, who have taught me a wealth of lessons and have nourished me with their enthusiasm and goodwill.

To conclude, APROQUEN continues in spite of everything, by the will of God and with the goodness and generosity of all our donors. We hope they and many new donors will join in the effort to promote this work since the funds raised from the sale of this book will be given to the burned children of an institution in every country where the book is sold.

The truth is, we must join efforts since, unfortunately, the reality of burned children persists at the same levels, not only in Nicaragua but in many places on the planet. This effort needs to be replicated and multiplied since it is clear we cannot do so without raising everyone's awareness.

My purpose has been and will be to devote myself fully to this cause until my last heartbeat. I will fight to alleviate the pain of burned children and to draw a smile on their faces so that hope shines in their eyes.

APPENDICES

"A planet without feelings would be a sad place as it would lead humanity to the path of despair and to the death of the spirit. At the end, we would become cold and selfish beings with no other motivation than personal benefit and material interest."

Vivian Pellas

Testimonials of Those Who Have Shared This Path

Vernon Guerrero

Vernon Guerrero has supported APROQUEN since its inception.

Laughing, he shares the following anecdote:

I once sent Vivian a check and asked her to keep it confidential.

Then she told me:

"Come in, I want to talk to you and ... please, can you bring a jacket?"

When I arrived, her words were:

"Please, put the jacket on and let's take a picture of us because we need the help of a hundred hearts like yours. Otherwise, aproquen will starve. We can't support the children only with you and Carlos. It won't work. We need a hundred like you!"

Today, Vernon considers himself a "loyal collaborator of APROQUEN" and gets so excited about it that tears fall from his eyes as he assures me that working with burned children has changed his life. In that regard, he affirms:

"A child's smile is worth more than anything because that smile goes straight to your soul and feeds your spirit. It is priceless. I've had two people who have made an impact on my life: one of them is my father with his example of love for others, and the other one is Vivian Pellas. I'm not the same since I found aproquen, and I feel very grateful for that."

Carlos Francisco Pellas

My mom is a lioness. She's strong, fights for her ideals, and takes care of us! I remember that she used to give me her blessing in bed at night before I went to sleep. We would say the Lord's Prayer together, and that made me feel safe. I always waited for those moments. She was the last person I saw before closing my eyes.

I remember my mom before the accident at the piñata parties. She had a cabin where she painted. I remember her as an artist. She painted shells, she painted birds.

My parents had the accident when I was ten. At that time, I was in Miami. I remember that I was in class and started to cry because several people asked me how my parents were doing. Nobody explained to me how serious the accident had been.

My maternal grandparents told me my mom had broken her arm, but I didn't know what was going on. Then I started crying, and the school principal showed me a newspaper that highlighted: "Banker Saves His Wife." That's how I found out.

I didn't recognize my mom when I first saw her after the accident. When I realized that it was her, I felt that she was very happy that we (my sister and I) were there by her side. I was scared when I saw her. Deep down, I knew I needed to be there for her.

When I walked into the hospital room, she was in bed and totally disfigured. I couldn't believe it was her. My sister ran out of the room crying, and I was left alone with my mom. That accident made me very strong and has shown me the enormous effort she has made for burned children.

Following the accident, I focused on my humanitarian side by founding, together with other friends, the "Hoy por Mañana" (Today for Tomorrow) Foundation, which helps children in need of school materials and other educational issues.

Family is the most important thing in life after God. It's important to be good and honest. The right way is to serve others, especially living in a country where there is so much poverty. This is my mother's teaching.

※

Vivian Vanessa Pellas

My mom is a simple and very strong woman with a big heart— sometimes too big—and that's why not-so-good things have happened to her. She always tries to see good in people. She has been betrayed as well, even by people she trusted and loved very much. She is a humble person who does not care about social classes, nor does she discriminate. She sees and treats everyone equally. She is honest, not hypocritical, and she doesn't care about what people think of her.

That's just the way she is.

Her way of being and thinking is as joyful as if she were a person my own age. And when it comes to energy level ... don't get me started, she just doesn't stop! She is extremely courageous with an enormous faith in God and is completely committed to her cause, which in addition to her family, is her reason for being and her mission in life.

Thanks to God, our family has been united and happy. Since I was a child, I have seen my parents respect, admire, love, and support each other in order to be better people. My parents are the people I admire the most: each one of them for different reasons but both equally. I feel happy and blessed to have them as role models and as parents and for having the brothers and the family that God has given me.

My mother's mission is between her and God. It's something intense that probably only she understands. It goes beyond what many of us can imagine.

Aproquen will continue, but there is only one Vivian Pellas.

※

Eduardo Pellas

To any child, talking about their mom is the easiest thing in the world. There are only nice words and infinite gratitude to be expressed. However, I would like to focus on two specific characteristics that describe my mom, and both of them have to do with her soul and her spirit.

The first one is that she transmits great positive energy. She spreads joy, sweetness, love, and humanity to others. For example, in the Christmas caravans and days of medical work where my mom visits thousands of patients, she manages, in an instant, to create a deep connection with people, leaving everyone she touches with a smile.

One of the most impressive moments I have experienced with her was when she inaugurated a park in the city of Chichigalpa. There were about 10,000 people, and I witnessed how my mom laughed, hugged, and talked to many of them. I don't know how to explain it, but I felt that she was connected to that crowd, and I was impressed by the feeling that her presence transmitted.

The second is that making others happy, especially those who need it most, makes her happy. She is devoted to others in a genuine and natural way. There is no question that helping is her passion, and she always puts others before herself by dedicating, and in some cases sacrificing, most of her life to support those in need.

It is difficult to explain these characteristics since they are intangible, but I believe that they are the engine behind all the social work she has done. I am convinced that her work, her dedication, and that special connection she has with people come from God.

I was only three years old when the accident happened. I was going to go on the flight, along with my parents, but due to a last-minute change, I didn't go with them ... thank God!

In particular, I remember three things about the accident. One of them was that I was not allowed to watch TV for a long time. Second, I have a memory of my mom leaving the hospital in a wheelchair and with a mask on her face. However, I didn't recognize her. And finally, I remember seeing that dad had a prosthesis on his hand. I didn't understand what had happened.

One of the things I have learned about the tragedy that my parents experienced is that life can be lost in *an instant. Therefore, we should not let small things affect us. The perseverance and dedication of my parents to fight (physically and psychologically) for their survival and to leave a great legacy has led me to feel great admiration for them.*

Thank you, mom, for being an inspiration in my life. Thank you for creating a better world with your great heart. The world needs more humane people like you.

César Estrada

César Estrada at his grocery shop in the Iván Montenegro market. Managua, Nicaragua, 2013.

You have made it possible for people like me to move forward and coexist with others without fearing the way they look at me and their judgment. I have opened myself up to the world and have no limits in my life. Regardless of my burns, I am not afraid of anything. You have filled a space that the burns had erased. Aproquen has given us love, attention, and very special care. You have supported me to the point of making me smile.

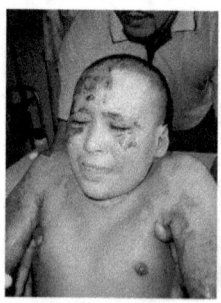 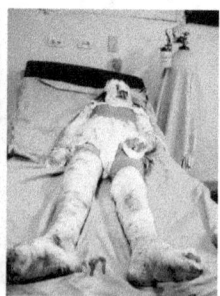

César Estrada suffered burns on January 2, 2004. Managua, Nicaragua.

Jimmy Rosales

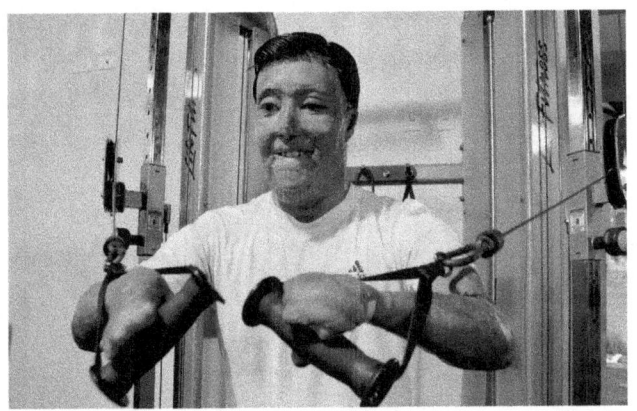

Jimmy Rosales at the gym. Managua, Nicaragua, 2016.

I suffered third-degree burns when I was only three years old. I arrived at aproquen, where I received all the medical attention I needed. Without them, I would not be where I am today. Aproquen was the means of salvation that God put in my life to turn my tears into smiles.

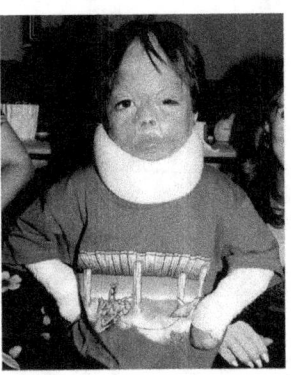

Jimmy, shortly after joining APROQUEN.

Mareling Alemán

Mareling Elizabeth Alemán Téllez. February 5, 2016.

APROQUEN is not only a non-profit organization that saved my life, it also saved my aching soul and those of my family from trauma. From aproquen, I have received love, affection, understanding, and, why not say, pampering.

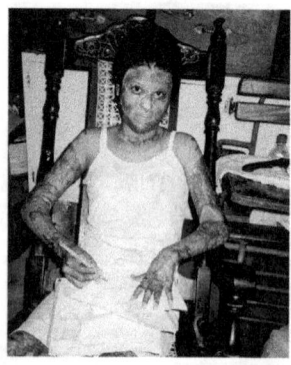

Mareling before her rehabilitation.

Miguel Ángel Carcache

We are nothing without your help and that of the doctors. However, since the Lord opened the doors for you and touched your hearts, you saved lives like mine and those of many children at APROQUEN. I'm grateful with all my heart that I'm alive.

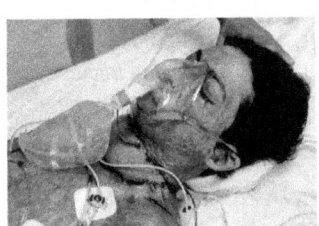

Miguel Ángel suffered burns on November 20, 2006.

And the endorsement of the experts:

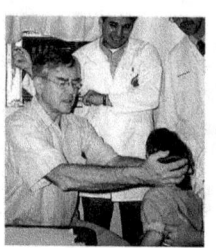

Dr. Anthony Wolfe, M.D., P.A.
Cranio-maxillofacial surgeon, disciple of Dr. Tessier, and creator of Cranio-maxillofacial Surgery. He is the Director of Plastic and Reconstructive Surgery at Nicklaus Children's Hospital in Miami, Florida.

"The work APROQUEN does is a piece of art."

Dr. Armand Versaci, M.D.
Pioneer of Plastic Surgery at Brown University

"It's an island of excellence and a university without frontiers."

Dr. Alberto Bolgiani
Expert in burn patients, Director of the ABIQ course ("Atención Básica Inicial del Quemado") - Federación Latinoamericana de Quemados.

"This is something wonderful and unprecedented in our Latin American countries."

Don Wagner, LFAHE
Former CEO Memorial Hermann Southwest Hospital

"APROQUEN'S *story and initiative caused a deep impression, not only on me but on our President and Board of Directors. There was unanimous agreement to provide them with all the help they requested. I had the honor of coordinating the advice and facilitating all the necessary links to provide technical assistance. Aproquen is the recognized leader in the region. The work of its excellent team is a Nicaraguan treasure."*

Dr. José Manuel Solla Camino
Primary care physician and former president of the Spanish General Medicine Association

"APROQUEN *is a charity that takes care of all kinds of burned people with no resources and operates in an enviable manner. Patients get their appointments immediately, and the care they receive couldn't be better. Dr. Mario Pérez, a plastic surgeon with extensive experience in the care of burn patients, is the director, but the follow-up is equally thorough with the intervention of pediatricians, psychologists, and physical therapists."*

Vivian receives the Servant of Peace Award from His Eminence, Archbishop Renato R. Martino, Permanent Observer of the Holy See to the United Nations.

Recognitions
Vivian Pellas's Memorable Moments

1992 *Aproquen's first artistic gala.*

1993 *Vivian Pellas inaugurates the first Burn Unit at the public Fernando Vélez Paiz Hospital.*

1999 *Servitor Pacis, bestowed upon Vivian Pellas by Apostolic Nuncio and Permanent Observer of the Vatican to the United Nations, Archbishop Renato R. Martino, on behalf of the Path to Peace Foundation of the Permanent Observer Mission of the Holy See to the United Nations.*

Honorary Doctorate from Ave María College. Managua, Nicaragua, 2002.

2002 *Honorary Doctorate. Ave María College, Nicaragua.*

2002 *June 1, Day of the Association for Burned Children of Nicaragua / Vivian Pellas Day, decreed by Raul L. Martínez, Mayor of the City of Hialeah, Miami, Florida.*

2004 *Inauguration of the Burn Unit, which is compliant with international standards and adjacent to Vivian Pellas Hospital.*

2004 *Recognition by the Ministry of Health in the First National Fair: Women, Health and Development.*

2004 *Recognition for the human rights of children and adolescents in Nicaragua by the Attorney General's Office for Human Rights (Procuraduría para la Defensa de Derechos Humanos-PDDH).*

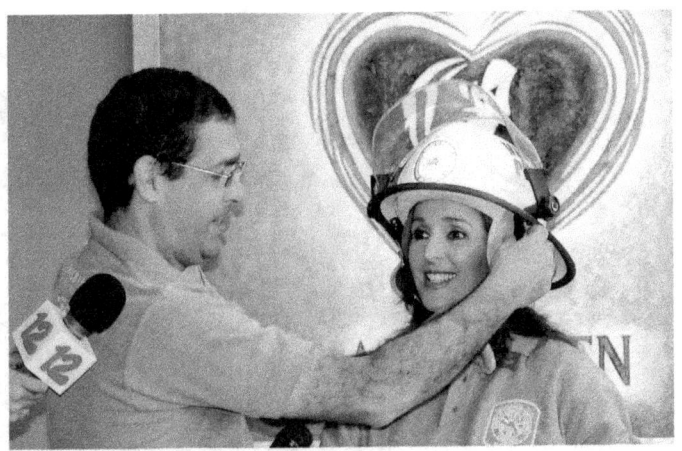

Appointment as Captain of the Civil Association, Volunteer Fire Department of Nicaragua, by the First Chief Commander of ACCBVN, Jaime Delgado. Vivian became the first woman to be appointed commander. Managua, Nicaragua, 2005.

2005 *Appointment as Captain of the Association of Volunteer Firefighters.*

2006 *Recognition by the United Nations Children's Fund (UNICEF).*

2006 *Recognition by the American Chamber of Commerce of Nicaragua (AMCHAM) for the children and population of Nicaragua.*

2007 *Main speaker at the 19th World Burn Congress. Vancouver, Canada.*

*Humanitarian Leader 2008.
Bravo Business Awards.
Latin Trade Magazine.
Miami, Florida, 2008.*

2008 *International magazine Latin Trade bestowed the BRAVO Business Award upon Vivian Pellas, recognizing her as the "Humanitarian Leader of the Year" on the continent.*

The winners of the other categories were: **Innovation**, Rubén Blades, Minister of Tourism of Panama; **Finance**, Henrique de Campos Meirelles, President of the Central Bank of Brazil; **President of the Year**, Enrique Cueto Plaza, President of LAN Airlines; International President, Subramaniam Ramadorai, President, Tata Consultancy Services; **Technology**, Marcelo Argüelles, President, Sidus Pharmaceutical Group; **Humanitarian Leader**, Vivian Pellas, Executive President of Asociación Pro Niños Quemados de Nicaragua; **Environmentalist**, Richard Hansen, President of the Foundation for Anthropological Research & Environmental Studies.

Grand Cross pro Merito Melitensi by the Knights of the Order of Malta. Presented by Monsignor Mauro Carlino, Secretary of the Apostolic Nunciature, who gave the award on behalf of His Excellency Nuncio Henryk Jozef Nowacki. Managua, Nicaragua, 2010.

2010 Grand Cross Pro Merito Melitensi by the Knights of the Sovereign Military Order of Malta, the highest honor conferred on a person who is not a member of the Order or a Head of State.

2010 Inauguration of the Lydia Fernández Rehabilitation Center in APROQUEN.

2011 "Nicaragua es" (Nicaragua Is) Award conferred by Citibank Nicaragua.

2012 Personality of the Year Award given by the Consejo Superior de Empresa Privada - COSEP (Superior Council of Private Enterprise).

2013 Integral Business Recognition by the Consejo Empresarial de América Latina - CEAL (Business Council of Latin America).

2013 Recognition by the Nicaraguan Medical Association.

2014 Henri Dunant Award for Corporate Social Responsibility, United States, by the Interamerican Institute for Democracy.

2014 Vivian received the keys to the city from James Cason, the Mayor of Coral Gables, Miami, Florida.

2015 Childhood Stars Award by World Vision Nicaragua.

2016 Fervent Love for Life Award by the Chou Ta-Kuan Foundation in Taiwan.

Vivian and Kim Phúc, known worldwide as the Napalm girl, a survivor of the Vietnam War. Vancouver, Canada, 2008.

Nicaragua Es (Nicaragua Is) Award given by Citibank Nicaragua, 2011.

Henri Dunant Award for Corporate Social Responsibility by the Interamerican Institute for Democracy, conferred by writer Armando Valladares Pérez and Carlos Alberto Montaner, writer and journalist. Miami, Florida, 2014.

Childhood Stars Award by World Vision Nicaragua, conferred by María Haydeé Pereira. Managua, Nicaragua, 2015.

Fervent Love for Life Award granted by the Chou Ta-Kuan Foundation in Taiwan, presented by Ambassador Rolando Jer-Ming Chuang, 2016.

Hall of Honor for Our Donors

To thank all of those who were always there for us. And of course, to thank all of those who continue to actively support us today.

My eternal gratitude to all of those who came, participated, and moved on.

My eternal gratitude to all of those who came, fell in love with this social work ... and stayed!

I don't know what aproquen or I would have done without you.

TITANIUM

- CLARO
- DICEGSA
- Vos Tv
- GBM Corporation
- Ron Flor de Caña
- La Nueva Radio Ya
- Hospital Vivian Pellas
- Sr. Ronald Rosenfeld
- Mosaico Audio Visual
- Direct Relief International
- Carlos Pellas Chamorro
- José Fernández (†)
- Supermercados La Colonia
- BAC Credomatic Network
- American Nicaraguan Foundation (ANF)
- Banco Centroamericano de Integración Económica (BCIE)

DIAMANTE

- Marc Stanley
- CEM JWT Comunicaciones

PLATINO

- Nicaragua Sugar Ltda.
- Donald B. Wagner
- Medical Bridges
- Sunshine Social Welfare Foundation (SSWF)

ORO

- Hasbro Latin America, INC
- D'guerrero Ingenieros S.A.
- Puma Energy Foundation
- Grupo Casa Pellas
- Sr. Curt Schaeffer
- Sra. Nena Pellas
- GGI Tuning
- OXFAM

PLATA

- Puma Energy Nicaragua
- NIMAC
- PWC Nicaragua
- Lydia Work
- Ilse Ortíz de Manzanares
- Adela Pellas de Solórzano
- Carisam-Samuel Meisel, Inc.
- David Flory
- E. Chamorro S.A.
- BAC Florida Bank
- Mukul Resort
- Guacalito de la Isla
- Children's Burn Foundation (CBF)
- Silvio Federico Pellas y Consuelo Martínez
- Dr. Danilo Manzanares
- Joe Clark
- Frank Robleto
- Joseph Dietch
- Roberto Kriete
- Francis Durman
- Ricardo Maduro
- Michael Wood

BRONCE

- Acco Terramar
- Greg Angel
- Edgar Ahlers
- BAC Panamá
- Diane Finnerty
- Seguros América, S.A.
- Ilse Manzanarez Brenner
- Compañía Cervecera de Nicaragua CCN
- Douglas Broderick/Patrick Broderick Memorial Foundation

CRISTAL

- My Father Cigars
- BAYER, S.A.
- ARGEÑAL & CIA
- Tabacalera Tambor, S.A.
- Johns Hopkins University
- Dr.Gilberto Martínez Acosta
- Leonora Solórzano de Pellas
- Dr. Jorge Enrique Castillo López
- Dr. Jaider Chavarría Altamirano
- Dr. Ernesto Anibal Salasblanca Rocha
- British American Tobacco Nicaragua
- Rosita Solorzano Pellas (†)
- Joseph Wolfe
- Juan José Domenech
- Mike & Megan Sihle
- Andrew and Ann Tisch
- Durman Esquivel, S.A.
- DHL Nicaragua S.A.
- Dr. Álvaro Fuentes
- Dra. Anneli Ahlers
- Grupo Münkel
- Silvio Solórzano Pellas

Illusions, for our Children, Year after Year

1992	Da un poquito de amor... Da un poquito de vida (Give a Little Love... Give a Little Life)
1993	Después de todo... es un mundo pequeño (After All... It's a Small World)
1994	Por la sonrisa de un niño (For a Child's Smile)
1995	Bailemos por la vida (Let's Dance for Life)
1996	¡Rompiendo la tradición! (Breaking with Tradition!)
1997	Segunda piel (Second Skin)
1998	¡Viviré! (I Will Live!)
1999	El amor nos une para un nuevo siglo (Love Unites Us for a New Century)
2000	Acrobacias, Sueños e Ilusiones (Acrobatics, Dreams and Illusions)
2001	El escenario es tu corazón (The Stage Is Your Heart)
2002	Un planeta de Ilusiones (A Planet of Illusions)
2003	Porque te tengo a ti (Because I Have You)
2004	Un sueño hecho realidad (A Dream Come True)
2005	La llave del Fénix (The Key of the Phoenix)
2006	15 años de película (15 Splendid Years)
2007	Son del Corazón (Music from the Heart)
2008	El Principito (The Little Prince)
2009	El Mago de Oz (The Wizard of Oz)
2010	Peter Pan
2011	Pinocho (Pinocchio)
2012	El Rey León, El Musical (The Lion King, The Musical)
2013	Mary Poppins, El Musical (Mary Poppins, The Musical)
2014	La Bella y la Bestia, El Musical (Beauty and the Beast, The Musical)
2016	Aladino, El Musical (Aladdin, The Musical)

My Life in Images

Vivian at the age of three with her five-year-old brother Alejandro. Havana, Cuba, 1957.

*Vivian at her birthday party, with family and friends.
Havana, Cuba, 1959.*

*Vivian at the age of fourteen studying guitar.
Managua, Nicaragua, 1968.*

Vivian at the age of fifteen. Managua, Nicaragua, 1970.

Sweethearts Carlos and Vivian. Managua, Nicaragua, 1975.

Vivian and her father on her wedding day at the Church of San Francisco. Managua, Nicaragua, 1976.

Carlos and Vivian.
San Juan del Sur, Nicaragua, 1977.

José Fernández with Dr. Edmundo del Carmen.
Tegucigalpa, Honduras, 1980.

*Vivian's mother and Carlos Francisco.
Managua, Nicaragua, 1983.*

*Vivian, her mother, and her son Carlos Francisco at
the age of one and a half. Miami, Florida, 1983.*

Carlos and his children, Carlos Francisco, Vivian Vanessa, and Eduardo. 1986.

Vivian, her mother Lydia Fernández, and her grandmother Isidora. Miami, Florida, 1986.

*Vivian and Carlos with their friends, Rogelia and William Zarruk.
Miami, Florida, 1987.*

*Vivian Vanessa and Eduardo.
Managua, Nicaragua, 1987.*

Eduardo at the age of two.
Managua, Nicaragua, 1988.

Vivian and her son Carlos Francisco.
San Juan del Sur, Nicaragua, 1983.

Vivian and Carlos with their children two months before the accident. Miami, Florida, 1989.

Carlos, his son Eduardo, and a sailfish that was later set free. Las Cocineras, Costa Rica, 1993.

Vivian, her parents, and her brother Alex at the Rubén Darío National Theater. Managua, Nicaragua, 1994.

Vivian and her daughter Vivian Vanessa during the Segunda Piel (Second Skin) Annual Gala. Managua, Nicaragua, 1997.

Monument to honor the victim's memory of the airplane accident of October 21, 1989, at Cerro de Hula. Tegucigalpa, Honduras.

*Vivian dancing flamenco with dancer William Herrera.
Managua, Nicaragua, 1998.*

The Pellas Family. From left to right: Francisco Alfredo and Theresita; Carlos and Vivian; Alfredo and Nena; Lucía and Felipe Mántica; Consuelo and Silvio. Granada, Nicaragua, 2002.

Vivian dancing at the Annual Gala Un Sueño hecho Realidad (A Dream Come True) Managua, Nicaragua, 2004.

*Carlos Francisco, Vivian's eldest son.
Managua, Nicaragua, 2007.*

*Vivian, her father, and her daughter at the Gala of aproquen's
performance of El Principito (The Little Prince) at the
Rubén Darío National Theater.
Managua, Nicaragua, 2008.*

Vivian at the Gala of the performance El Mago de Oz (The Wizard of Oz). Managua, Nicaragua, 2009.

Vivian and her daughter Vivian Vanessa at the 2010 Annual Gala. Peter Pan at the Rubén Darío National Theater. Managua, Nicaragua.

Vivian and her daughter Vivian Vanessa, at aproquen's Annual Gala Aladino, El Musical (Aladdin The Musical) at the Rubén Darío National Theater. Managua, Nicaragua, 2016.

My grandchildren: Sienna Nicole, Vivian Isabella and Juan Carlos. Mukul Resort, Guacalito de la Isla, Nicaragua, 2017.

My grandchildren Pietro, Nicolás, Lorenzo and Joaquin, 2025

My grandchild: Valentina Marie Pellas De Smet at 8 months old.

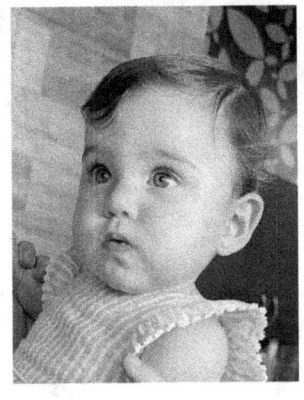

Vivian during an educational activity in which school materials and gifts were given to the children. Cerro de Chipote, Quilalí, Nueva Segovia, Nicaragua, 2003.

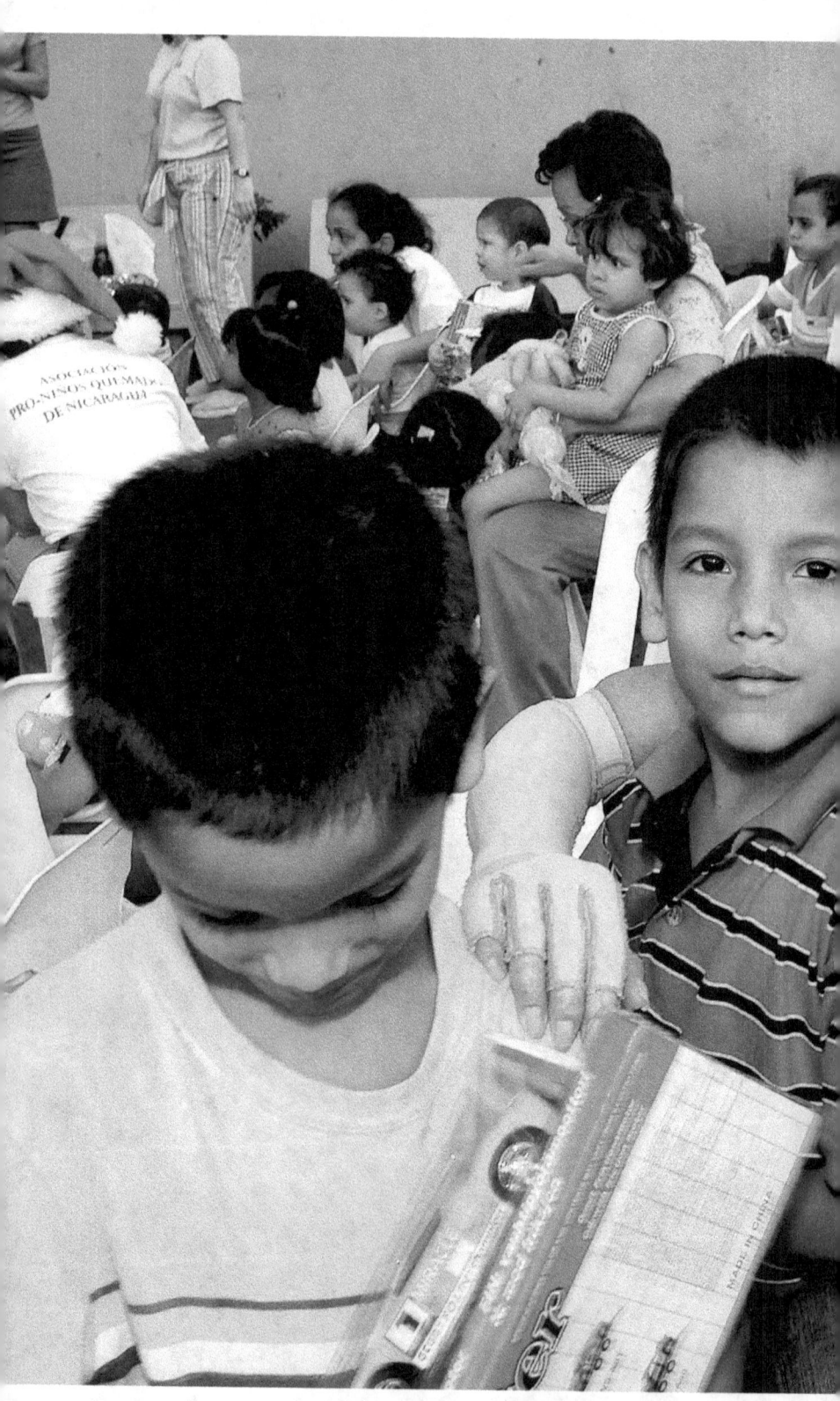

*Delivery of toys, APROQUEN'S Christmas Caravan.
Managua, Nicaragua, 2018.*

Delivery of toys. Quilalí, Nueva Segovia, Nicaragua, 2003.

Vivian with rehabilitated aproquen children.
El Crucero, Nicaragua, 2015.

My Immense Gratitude ...

To my FAMILY, especially my children, Carlos Francisco, Vivian Vanessa, and Eduardo, for the time they dedicated to this book.

To Carlos, for his great love and for respecting and supporting my decisions.

To Juan Carlos, Milena, and Daniela, for the joy they have brought to the family. And to all of those who dedicate their time and work to aproquen.

And to our very generous and altruistic donors that make our existence possible.

TO THE UNCONDITIONAL

- Dr. Mario Pérez
- Xiomara Argeñal
- Héctor Gaitán
- Grethel Guevara
- Dennis Schwartz Arce
- Dr. Humberto Briceño
- Gisella Rodríguez

TO THE VOLUNTEERS

- María Jesús Lacayo
- Sr. César Espinoza
- Lenin Frixione
- Stefania Félez
- Dr. René Ruíz
- Edda Magaly
- Deyanira Argüello
- Dra. María Belinda Bendaña
- Dra. Zela Porras
- Evelyn Murillo
- Dra. Julia Mena
- Dra. Daysi Masís
- Carmen Urrutia
- Martín Medina
- Alba Roni Aguilar
- Dra. Ivette Icaza
- Dennis Schwartz Galo
- Mariell Riguero
- Miriam Lacayo
- Isolda Mayorga
- Iralia Sandino

- Griselle Villavicencio
- Olimpia Barcenas
- Connie Lacayo
- Dra. Annely Ahlers
- Jorge Delgado
- Sara Reed
- Jen Gottlieb
- Chris Winfield

TO THE INTERNATIONAL ALLIES

- Dr. Armand Versaci (†)
- Dr. Gary Brody
- Dr. Rick Sieller
- Dr. Nicholas Namais
- Dr. Anthony Wolfe
- Dra. Marta Mejía
- Dr. David Harrington
- Dr. Phillip Freshwater
- Dr. Robert Sheridan
- American Burn Association (ABA)
- International Society of Burn Injuries
- ReSurge International
- Brown University
- Memorial Hermann Hospital
- 740 Park Plastic Surgery
- Physicians for Peace
- SOS Main du Pays D'aix en Provence
- Sunshine Social Welfare Foundation
- PUMA Energy Foundation
- Johns Hopkins University School of Medicine
- Greater Baltimore Medical Center
- Emory University
- Loma Linda University
- Smile Train
- ORPHANetwork
- Seeds for the Progress
- Fabretto Foundation
- Jackson Memorial Hospital
- Dr. Stafford Broumand, N.Y

ADVISORY BOARD

- Al Germi
- Curt Schaeffer
- Jorge Latorre
- Kimberly Goldfien
- Dr. Stafford Broumand
- Mike Wood
- Dr. Patrick Byrne
- Marc Stanley
- Frank Robleto
- Ilse Manzanares
- Don Wagner

TO THOSE WHO MADE A CONTRIBUTION TO APROQUEN WITH THEIR TALENT AND ENTHUSIASM AT THE GALAS

- Donaldo Aguirre
- Xiomara Argeñal
- Dennis Schwartz Arce
- Jacobo and Xiora Martínez
- Martín Medina
- Elvin Vanegas
- Ricardo López ("Camarita")

TO ALL OF THOSE WHO HAVE SUPPORTED THIS BOOK

- Salvador Espinoza
- Dennis Schwartz Arce
- Xiomara Argeñal Baltodano
- Grethel Guevara
- Mairym Cruz Bernal

I have made an effort to fulfill my mission and my legacy. This book will travel to many places and will help an organization that provides care to children with burns in every country where it is sold. I dedicate this work of love to all the burned children of the world.

Vivian Pellas

Bogotá, D.C., February 11, 2020

Thank you ...
For my normal limbs,
while so many are mutilated;
For my perfect eyes,
while so many do not see the light;
For my voice that sings,
while others fall silent;
For my hands that work,
while others beg;
For being able to come home at the end of a day of work, while others don't have anywhere to go back to;
Because I am able to smile, love, dream, and live, while many cry, hate, and are troubled by nightmares ... and die while living;
Thank You, Lord,
because I have so little to ask for
and so much to be thankful for.

****Thanksgiving Day Prayer**
Anonymous

** Prayer read by Vivian Pellas at the first Thanksgiving Mass after returning to Managua, 1990.

"My purpose has been and will be to dedicate up to my last effort to this cause. I will fight until my final heartbeat to alleviate the pain of burned children."

Vivian Pellas – Turning Tears into Smiles was originally printed in April 2021 at the graphic studio of Quad/Graphics Colombia S.A.,
at Cl 17 No. 41-34, Bogotá, Colombia.
5,000 copies were printed.

Pellas, Vivian
   Vivian Pellas: Turning tears into smiles | Vivian Pellas; Author of the Prologue,
Carlos Pellas; Bogotá: Cangrejo Editores, 2021.
   376 pages: illustrations, photographs; 24 cm.
   Table of contents included.

   ISBN 978-958-5532-33-5

        1. Pellas, Vivian -- Personal stories 2. Airplane accidents – Testimonies
   3. Self-realization (Psychology) 4. Airplane accident survivors I. Pellas, Carlos,
   Author of the prologue III. Tít. IV. Series
   920 cd 22 ed.
   A1647950

           CEP-Banco de la República-Biblioteca Luis Ángel Arango

aproquen
Turning Pain into Purpose

PROVIDE HOPE FOR A CHILD TODAY.

APROQUEN is dedicated to providing philanthropic support to children vulnerable to or suffering from burns and/or cleft lip and palate across Latin America.

AproquenKids.org

THIS BOOK IS PROTECTED INTELLECTUAL PROPERTY

The author of this book values Intellectual Property. The book you just read is protected by Instant IP[IP], a proprietary process, which integrates blockchain technology giving Intellectual Property "Global Protection." By creating a "Time-Stamped" smart contract that can never be tampered with or changed, we establish "First Use" that tracks back to the author.

Instant IP[IP] functions much like a Pre-Patent since it provides an immutable "First Use" of the Intellectual Property. This is achieved through our proprietary process of leveraging blockchain technology and smart contracts. As a result, proving "First Use" is simple through a global and verifiable smart contract. By protecting intellectual property with blockchain technology and smart contracts, we establish a "First to File" event.

Protected by Instant IP[IP]

LEARN MORE AT INSTANTIP.TODAY

www.ingramcontent.com/pod-product-compliance
Lightning Source LLC
Chambersburg PA
CBHW072144070526
44585CB00015B/997